D1491332

Garden Graces

Garden Graces

The Wisdom in Growing Things

by Janice Elsheimer

BEACON HILL PRESS
OF KANSAS CITY

Printed in the
United States of America

Cover Design: J.R. Caines
Inside Design: Sharon Page
Cover and Inside Illustrations: Redenta Soprano

Library of Congress Cataloging-in-Publication Data

Elsheimer, Janice.
   Garden graces : the wisdom in growing things / Janice Elsheimer.
     p. cm.
   Includes bibliographical references.
   ISBN 978-0-8341-2493-6 (pbk.)
   1. Gardeners—Religious life. 2. Gardening—Religious aspcets—Christianity. 3. Gardens—Religious aspects—Christianity. I. Title.
   BV4596.G36E47 2010
   248.8'8—dc22

                                    2009045262

10 9 8 7 6 5 4 3 2 1

To my mother,
Phyllis Rose Hill Boosey (1926–2004),
who bequeathed me her passion for gardening

Contents

Preface

This book has been germinating most of my life; I couldn't have written it when I was younger. The lessons I've learned from gardening for the past thirty years needed time to take root. The Book of Proverbs tells us that wisdom "is more precious than rubies. . . . Her ways are pleasant ways, and all her paths are peace. She is a tree of life to those who embrace her; those who lay hold of her will be blessed" (Proverbs 3:15, 17-18). Gardening as a spiritual practice has afforded me much of the wisdom I've gained in my more than five decades of life. This book is an attempt to share some of that wisdom with others.

Garden Graces was not written sequentially, nor does it have to be read that way. You will notice that beginning with chapter one, "Golden Dewdrop," every third chapter has the name of a plant as its title, and it will lead you through the day from dawn until dark. After each plant chapter are two chapters dealing with gardening tasks. These chapters contain reliable gardening information and insights that I've picked up over the years and that I hope will help you in your own gardening endeavors. Each of these task chapters is also a metaphor for some aspect of life that most of us struggle with in our efforts to grow personally and spiritually. The final section of every task chapter offers you something to think about or do in order to apply the truth of the chapter to your life.

Margaret Silf writes in the foreword to Vigen Guroian's *Inheriting Paradise: Meditations on Gardening*, "Every suburban flower garden and every rural allotment has the potential of a two-way mirror: to bring eternity right down into our own backyard, and to open up in our own small worlds something of the very mind and heart of God."[1] I hope that somewhere in the pages of this book you'll find yourself looking into that two-way mirror as you come to recognize what gardeners already know in their bones—that nowhere else do we experience the oneness between the Creator and creation as intimately as we do in the garden.

Acknowledgments

From the beginning, my writers' critique group at Northland Church, Word Weavers, helped me prune this book into shape, fearlessly deadheading and weeding away, while still watering my writer's fragile ego with encouragement.

To Jan Richardson, Louise Sheehy, and Stacy Barton, thanks for your honesty, compassion, and willingness to give me the tough love I needed when the words started rambling like peppermint all over the place and had to be cut back.

Thanks to Janice Morgan and Patricia Schoene for listening to my readings and for being gardening buddies since the Arkansas days. And to Mona, my night-blooming cereus: thank you for your story.

To the people of Mountainburg, Arkansas, who taught me how to grow food and flowers in that rocky soil and then showed me how to share the bounty, I want to express my sincere appreciation.

And to all the Winter Park, Florida, neighbors I now call friends, thanks for taking time to stop by the garden and admire it with me. I especially want to thank Redenta Soprano, who spoke first that morning, exclaiming, "What a happy garden you have!" and who continues to praise and encourage all my creative efforts, both in and out of the garden.

And finally, to my husband, Seth, whose interests and talents lie outside the garden, thank you for being such an undemanding guy so that I get to do what makes me feel the most productive: staying grounded in the garden.

1

Golden Dewdrop
Duranta repens

A gardener does not grow from seed, shoot, bulb,
rhizome, or cutting, but from experience,
surroundings, and natural conditions.
—Karel Capek, *The Gardener's Year*

It's 7:00 A.M. and still dark outside. October in Florida doesn't arrive in full color with frosty cold snaps, but the feel of night well into morning is one sure sign of the changing seasons. I know this darkness sits on the edge of dawn, but it seems awfully late for it to be hanging around.

Not that I mind: light or dark, early morning is the best time of day for me. I've been up since five, have done some writing, and have been to the gym. No, I'm not a morning maniac. I just know how my mind and body rhythms work, and I try to use that knowledge to my benefit. As the day moves on, my energy and enthusiasm for even my favorite kind of work begin to fade. Best to start early and pack as much into the hours before noon as I can.

I go into my garden at all times of day, even when "mad dogs and Englishmen" are the only ones who might see me there. One reason I garden, in fact, is that it gives me an excuse to leave the house, breathe fresh air, and be out in the natural world. So I have a tendency to go to the garden off and on throughout the day and evening, hot or cold, rainy or clear.

Each time of day paints a different picture in the garden. From barely dawn to morning mist; from pastel pink and gold daybreak skies to sun-dance glitter on dewdrops to bright mid-day's short, sharp shadows on the lawn; from hazy afternoon stillness to the cool breath of sunset; from twilight to dark—the garden is an ever-changing work of art.

Even so, I like being outdoors at first light best of all. Ghost-ly shapes take on solid forms, and faded leaves and flowers resolve themselves into focus. Whites and other pastel shades perform this negative-to-positive transformation first and most distinctly. The pale, lavender-flowered shrub datura, or "gold-en dewdrop," comes shimmering into view before many of its darker-hued neighbors, greeting the dawn with its spindly, sky-ward-reaching branches.

Two golden dewdrop bushes crouch down among some tall white "Natchez" crape myrtles that line the curb along one side of my garden. When the golden dewdrops are blooming, delicate sprays of pale violet, bee-attracting blossoms dangle from the end of each branch. The woody shrub gets its common name from the gold berries that form after the small white-edged flowers have bloomed and fallen away. Because of its name, I associate the plant with my favorite time of day: the golden hour of dawn, when most living things are still asleep and those of us who are afoot can be alone in the coolness and silence of daybreak.

The golden dewdrop is not the first flower to awaken in the morning, but its name draws us into the gardener's day. When the dew lies on the lawn and the light is barely enough to see by,

I go to the garden alone. As often as not, the music of that old hymn comes to mind, and I pray.

I come to the garden alone,
While the dew is still on the roses;
And the voice I hear,
Falling on my ear,
The Son of God discloses.
And He walks with me, and He talks with me,
And He tells me I am His own;
And the joy we share as we tarry there,
None other has ever known.

—C. Austin Miles

I don't claim to hear God's voice in my ear, but I do believe that when I pray, God hears my voice and sends His Spirit to inspire, counsel, and direct me. I know that when I begin my day in prayer, especially if that prayer is connected to some creative act like writing in my journal or working in my garden, God fulfills His promise to "hear my voice."

One psalmist wrote, "In the morning, O LORD, you hear my voice; in the morning I lay my requests before you and wait in expectation" (Psalm 5:3). When I'm out in the garden, whether sitting on a bench with a cup of coffee, writing in my journal—which is one way I lay my requests before God—or down on my knees weeding, I feel a kinship with the writer of that psalm. I know what made him choose those words: it's the sense that in the morning you're as close to God as you can get.

Think about it. How bold it is to presume that God is waiting for us to speak to Him, to lay our requests before Him, and to wait in expectation while He fulfills them! Yet when we put ourselves into a setting that's as close to God's original design for us as we can get in this world—in a garden—we are emboldened. We do feel a kinship and intimacy with God that's hard to come by in the rush and busyness of the rest of the day. And that intimacy allows us to listen more keenly and to speak more courageously the longings and concerns of our hearts.

Author and theologian Franky Schaeffer has written a great deal about how using our artistic talents is a calling to make the world a more beautiful place while developing ourselves as spiritual beings. "What can be more spiritual," he writes, "in this sad and often ugly world than the creation of beauty?" He goes on: "True spirituality is . . . effecting change in the real world, not hiding behind religious experience."[1] Our duty, then, as artists who have a love for gardening, is to cultivate that gift and, in doing so, to engage in the creation of beauty in "this sad and often ugly world."

The earth is the gardener's canvas, and the arrangement, care, and cultivation of all the elements in the garden constitute the gardener's medium, the gardener's art form. All art begins with inspiration, the breathing in of ideas, visions, and energy from the Spirit of God, who is the Master Creator of the universe. When we "come to the garden alone, while the dew is still on the roses," we start our day in quiet and meditative expectation. We offer our talents and present our willingness to engage in this hard but satisfying work. Then we wait in expectation for that inspiration, not only for how we should garden but also for how we should live. As co-creators with God, we can rest assured that the inspiration will come.

So let's begin before the sunrise, with the golden dewdrop, lovely lady of the morning, reminding us that each day brings with it a new opportunity to give voice to our hopes and to wait in expectation for the God of all creation to reply.

2

Clearing a Space

*The garden must be prepared in the soul first, or
else it will not flourish. Tickle it with a hoe,
and it will laugh into a harvest.*
—old English proverb

I was nine years old the first time I asked my father if I could plant a garden "to grow some flowers and carrots." My family was moving to Indianapolis from Louisville, Kentucky, and I knew that one of the places I would miss most when we left was Wallitch Nursery. Wallitch's ran the length of our street, between Willmar Avenue and Carol Road, and we kids had to walk through it to get from one neighborhood to the next. Truth be told, there were ways to go around it, but who wanted to? From the mountains of mulch and well-composted manure perfect for scaling and sliding down, to the ancient weeping willow with its ready provision of "whips" shading the entrance to a glass-and-steel greenhouse, the nursery was a place of irresistible wonder. By the time we had left Louisville and Wallitch's behind, I was hooked on what would become my lifetime passion for growing things. I endured the move north on the strength of my father's promise to help me clear a space in our new backyard for a garden of my own.

Dad—ever the engineer—measured off a small plot about four feet wide and eight feet long, drove wooden stakes into each corner, and looped a line of twine from one stake to the next, outlining the garden's perimeter. He then showed me how to turn over the grass with a shovel. Although I was a tough little girl, this task defeated me. No matter how I tried to cut through that Indiana sod the way my father showed me, I couldn't make it happen. After watching me several times raise the shovel, my foot on its edge, and bring it down with a clatter only to have it impotently glance off the turf, Dad came to my rescue and dug up the rest of the plot for me while I watched. It was one of my first lessons in the use of leverage, and I gained a new respect for height and strength that day.

My next assignment was to shake the soil from the roots of the grass clumps he had dug up and then put the grass, weeds, and roots into a bucket to be hauled away. This was tedious work. I guess I expected the soil to be as loose and friable as the potting soil in those brown papier-mâché pots at Wallitch Nursery, but what I encountered was heavy, black Indiana clay. I didn't know the difference between commercial planting media and just plain yard dirt, but I soon learned. The Indiana soil I had to work with, albeit black and rich to look at, was heavy and tenacious in its hold on the roots of each little wedge of grass. But little by little, I removed all the grass and ended up with a clear and lovely patch of earth, my first garden.

I'm more than fifty years older now and several gardens wiser, yet I still turn over a new garden much the way my father taught me back in 1959. Not being enamored of rectangles, I tend to mark out my curvy borders with a garden hose rather than stakes and string, but otherwise the process is still the same. I've owned several garden tillers and even a tractor once upon a time, and those machines can certainly make clearing land easier on the front end. Technology has a place in even the most humble garden. But here at my home in central Florida, I've come full circle and clear the land the old-fashioned way: I turn it.

Turning over sod with a shovel, then leveling the soil with a bow rake, is still the best way I know to clear a space for a new bed or border. Using hand tools may require more initial energy, but it gives you control over what you're taking away and what you're leaving alone. It can actually be more time-efficient than using a tiller, because when we till, we turn the weeds—roots, seeds, and all—right back into the soil we're trying to clear. This does add organic matter to the soil, but it doesn't leave a clean slate, a truly cleared piece of land, to work with. The only way to make sure you're starting with nothing but good, loamy dirt is to turn over the sod a shovel load at a time and shake out the soil from the unwanted roots as you remove them, weeds and all.

Staying Grounded

When I'm engaged in a mindless activity like turning over shovel loads of sod and dirt, it becomes a form of meditation. The task itself requires very little thought, just concentration and care. This frees me to think about the wonder of what I'm doing, the wonder of this natural world God has seen fit to place me in. As I turn over the sod, I think about turning over more and more of my life to God.

The soul is like a garden, and what grows there is directly related to what kind of care we give it. The more we focus on our relationship with God, the more beautiful, productive, and energy-yielding that relationship becomes. As we work a new piece of earth, we can use these repetitive tasks as a form of con-templation, a form of prayer. As we turn over the sod to reveal the soil underneath, we can remind ourselves to turn over our lives and our wills to God so that we can discover the authentic person each of us was created to be.

If we want to grow as spiritual beings, we must not only turn over our lives to God but also make the space for new growth to occur. We have to do the work of uprooting those weeds that encroach upon the growth we want to nourish in order to start out clean and keep our efforts focused. Whenever I'm cutting through a tightly woven mat of St. Augustine, I'm doing away with one layer so that another can grow in its place. Each time we focus on an area of personal or spiritual growth, we should start by removing the old layer of bad habits and counterproductive behaviors that are choking out our attempts to bring new growth to fruition.

Soul Gardening

Where do you need to clear a space in your life so you can draw closer to God and see what plans He has "to prosper you and not to harm you"? (Jeremiah 29:11). What layers of protection—unnecessary busyness, nonproductive work habits, or old patterns that leave you depleted rather than energized—do you need to dig up, shake free of dirt, and send to the compost pile so you can make room for new spiritual growth?

Most of us could live with fewer material possessions, fewer time commitments, and less stuff to maintain. Everything we own exacts a price in time and maintenance. Spiritually mature people understand that the number of possessions they can live without, rather than the number they feel they are entitled to own, is the measure of true riches. If we want to make room for spiritual growth, we must be willing to clear a space in our busy lives so that growth can occur. As we turn over that busyness to the Creator God, whose only desire is to draw us closer to himself, we give ourselves the chance to grow into the people we're capable of becoming.

3

Enriching the Soil

If I make no other point in these pages,
let this message be clear:
nothing, but nothing matters as much
as soil preparation.
—James Underwood Crockett, *Crockett's Victory Garden*

I live in Florida, aptly named "land of flowers" by the Spaniards who appropriated the land from its native residents in the sixteenth century. Here the *conquistadores* found exotic plants flowering year round. Our semitropical climate, ample rainfall, and sandy, phosphorus-rich soil all contribute to the abundance of plant life in this peninsular state. For millions of years, biologists say, spent flora has settled on the forest floor beneath the huge trees and vines that once canopied most of the state. Guano from millions of birds and other tree dwellers heated up the detritus. Burrowing and digging animals mixed this mash, and with the help of rain and wind, the perfect medium for growing things was created: rich, loamy soil.

Florida, like most of the other states where forests once ruled the land and skies, was a naturally fertile place before overdevelopment, wetland draining, and phosphorus mining left much of it barren and wasted. It was here in Florida that I first learned to replicate nature by adding organic material to whatever soil I had to work with.

Soil is not just a medium for keeping plants upright; it is the vital organ that nourishes each plant and determines its health and well-being. Before we plant the first seed in the ground, we need to do the "groundwork." Whatever type of soil we've been blessed or cursed with, our first job is always soil-building.

Soils are usually classified by the size of particles that comprise their makeup. Clays have the smallest particles and are the densest; sandy soils have the largest particles and are the loosest.

When a handful of clay is squeezed in the hand, it tends to clump together in what looks a lot like potter's clay: slick and heavy when wet, adobe hard when dry. The tightly knit microscopic particles in clay soils make it hard for roots to penetrate and for oxygen and water to pass through freely. Clay is generally fertile, however, because of all the minerals it contains, and once it's loosened and made more friable by adding lots of organic material, it can acquire the texture gardeners look for in their best garden soils.

Sandy soils have the largest particles, and water and oxygen have no trouble passing through their loose, open spaces. This ease of passage makes it easy to work, but it allows nutrients to leach out of it continually. Sandy soils, like what we have here in Florida, can become infertile very quickly. One reason farmers drained vast stretches of what was once the Everglades was because of the dark, rich layer of muck at the bottom of these marshes and swamps—the result of eons of organic matter decomposing beneath the "river of grass."

Since sandy soils won't hold water long, plants and their roots are in danger of drying out during times of insufficient rainfall. In order for sandy soils to retain what moisture they do get, gardeners must add a great deal of organic matter. Just as with clay soil, sandy soils must be enhanced with generous amounts of humus, compost, and other soil amendments to turn them into an ideal planting medium.

Loamy soil represents a perfect compromise between clay and sand. It offers the fertility of clay with the aeration of sand. Loam retains moisture but drains rapidly enough to keep plant roots from rotting. Loamy soil is easy to dig, plant, and weed, and it contains most of the nutrients plants need to grow and thrive. Loam is what we're attempting to create and continually build in our gardens.

To build loamy soil we must add all kinds of organic matter, and this is where the scrounger gardener has a real advantage over the one who wouldn't dream of asking a neighbor to dump his or her leaves and grass clippings onto the compost pile. When I was in my twenties, I collected cow manure and shoveled out neighbors' chicken houses for manure to heat up my compost pile. I brought home three-pound cans of coffee grounds from the café where I worked summers as a waitress and dumped them either into the compost or directly into the garden. I begged bales of rotting hay from farmers who were happy to have me take them off their hands. Tree-trimming crews would dump huge loads of chipped limbs, leaves, and bark next to my garden, and what began as a twelve-foot mountain would break down into a four-foot molehill of mulch by the following season.

Each year I would till the previous year's layer of mulch into the garden, where it would continue to break down and enrich my soil. Then I would layer last year's mellowed pile of tree trimmings onto the garden, where it became the present year's mulch. And the process goes on and on, just as in the forest primeval.

The more you're aware of all the organic material that's out there free for the picking, the more you'll notice it and see its virtue as a soil enhancer. Gardeners tend to see connections in all of life; recognizing how what would otherwise go to the county landfill can become a soil enhancer in the garden not only is practical but also has a kind of wisdom about it. Rumpelstiltskin could spin straw into gold; we can turn trash into a treasure trove of "black gold"—soil-enhancing humus.

Of course, for those of us who are past our manure-shoveling prime or who simply don't have access to such free materials, there are folks who, for a small price, will gladly deliver spoiled hay, topsoil, composted cow manure, and other soil enhancers directly to our gardens. But all of us can compost our garden and kitchen wastes, our raked leaves and grass clippings, and continue to build our garden soil with materials that would otherwise be wasted.

Good, rich soil is what we get when we make the most of what we're given. Stuart Maddox Masters wrote,

Soil . . . scoop up a handful of the magic stuff. Look at it closely. What wonders it holds as it lies there in your palm. Tiny sharp grains of sand, little faggots of wood and leaf fiber, infinitely small round pieces of marble, fragments of shell, specks of black carbon, a section of vertebrae from some minute creature. And mingling with it all, the dust of countless generations of plants and flowers, trees, animals and—yes— our own, age-long forgotten forebears, gardeners of long ago. Can this incredible composition be the common soil?[1]

What Masters is describing is loam, exactly what we're striving to create when we enhance whatever soil we have to work with.

When crops are deprived of basic nutrients, they languish. Organic soil amendments and conditioners pay for themselves with increased plant productivity. Healthy plants grow more vigorously, taste better, store longer, and better resist insect attacks. They have greater resistance to the cold, heat, drought, and disease. Successful soil building best addresses the soil's long-term needs by remedying deficiencies organically.[2]

Soil enriched with humus, manures, and compost changes its look, feel, and smell immediately upon application.

If we think of gardening as making the world a better place to live—our attempt to give something back—then it's important that we consider ourselves not just caretakers but developers of the soil in our gardens. It's our little contribution to eternity right here on earth. This starts with soil-building.

Staying Grounded

Good gardeners enrich their soil in preparation for planting. If we don't do the work up front, we'll pay for it in spindly plants, dried-out soil that needs constant watering, and an overall puny garden. We'll still have to do the work later on—fertilizing and mulching more frequently, weeding more often, replacing plants that don't make it in infertile soil—and our garden will never be as verdant and healthy as it would have been had we enriched the soil properly at the beginning.

Likewise, living a rich, meaningful life begins with building our base. Those who live atop a foundation of shifting values and ever-changing ideals and beliefs are destined to struggle more in establishing themselves. I know—I learned this lesson the hard way. I started my adult life with no more belief in God than a vague notion that a creative force had set things in motion and then sat back and watched them unfold, so I had nothing to hold me up when the winds of life started blowing me over.

Now that I recognize that God is real and present and interested in my well-being, I have that rich and fertile foundation in which to grow. I've raised my son in this fruitful ground, and although he's struggling with his own young adult beliefs, I know that the firm foundation he grew up in will hold him up and enrich his life in spite of any doubts he may be having right now.

As you enrich your garden soil, you might think about free or inexpensive ways to enhance the rest of your life. Maybe you spend more time than you would like envying your wealthier friends with their beach condos, their European vacations, and all the exciting things they can afford to do. Instead of coveting their lives, try focusing on ways to enrich your life without having to get into debt. You can redirect that envy energy into finding inexpensive or free ways to have meaningful family, couple, or personal adventures. Day hikes, camping trips, or weekends at cabins in state parks can be wonderful ways to draw family and friends closer together, and these activities can cost very little.

In addition to the occasional trip or outing, you can plan for inexpensive family projects right at home. You might be surprised to see how dumping a colorful jigsaw puzzle onto a card table can bring the family together.

Soul Gardening

Make a deal with yourself to stop cutting corners in life. Do the work you need to do at the beginning of any project, because if you don't, you'll regret it when you see that the project doesn't succeed. Growing personally and spiritually, like building up your soil, requires attention, time, and effort. You can't build a solid life on ideals that change with the fashion of the day or with your newest group of friends. Decide what you really believe about how God functions in your life, and cultivate your relationship with Him. Enrich it with prayer, with doing the next right thing and with giving time and resources to those who are in greater need than you. Build your foundation, and as the seasons of your life pass, that foundation will grow stronger.

4

Morning Glory
Ipomoea purpurea

*Well-named morning glory. Its broad bell and
trumpet-shaped flowers, faintly tinged with red,
are like the dawn itself.*
—Henry David Thoreau, *Journals*

As I've already admitted, I'm one of those odd and sometimes irritating morning people. I like waking in the dark and watching the sky grow gradually lighter. I love walking through dew-moist grass even if it means getting my shoes wet. I like the way the morning air feels cool and fresh on my skin. If I hope to accomplish anything of value in a day, I had better start in the early morning. During our sweltering Florida summers, morning is as cool as it's likely to get, and staying indoors makes absolutely no sense to me when the grandeur of the morning awaits just outside the door.

Besides, this is the only time of day when I can admire the morning glories. Although morning glories come in shades of purple, pink, white, and even red, "heavenly blue" is the one I love most. This variety of *Ipomoea-purpurea* is considered a tri-color because of the white and yellow throat at the center of its blue petals, but what people walking by see is a trellis that's covered in the purest sky blue I've yet to find in the plant kingdom. When the sun crests the huge laurel oaks on the east side of our property, "heavenly blue" is the only way to describe the trumpets that hug my south-facing garden wall, climbing up both sides of the arched lanai to welcome the new day. How could I stay in bed and miss their glorious opening each morning?

The large, fragrant flowers of the morning glory, some as big as four inches in diameter, unfold to greet the morning sun and then close up in the afternoon. They entwine themselves around trellises, lampposts, fences, and nearby plants. They'll cover an ugly utility pole, its guy wires, even a brush pile, because even after the blossoms close up, the leaves form a solid, living screen of privacy. Wild *Ipomoea*, called bindweed, are just as pretty, but they're much too invasive to plant in my garden. I content myself with seeing them on my morning walk, where they serve as a groundcover over infertile sandy soil, transforming a blanket of dead trees into fountains of purple, magenta, blue, and green.

Native to the tropics, more than two hundred species of morning glories come from the Americas alone. Morning glories grow from seeds and reseed freely, so they can overrun your garden if you're not careful. The planting instructions on most seed packets recommend that the gardener either soak these hard-shelled seeds in warm water for a couple of hours to soften them before planting or nick each seed with a knife to increase the germination rate. It's hard for me to believe that one needs to go through all that since they reseed so freely that they can become a problem if left unchecked. Still, it's probably a good idea to follow the packet's directions. Then stand back.

Once your morning glories are established, they should grow well even if left unattended. Soil should be kept moist but not wet. During dry periods water them once or twice a week and mulch around them to keep weeds down and improve appearance. Their requirements are few, and their daily crop of freshly opened flowers makes them one of the most widely grown of all annual vines.

One final story about these glorious climbers: in a study on morning glories, researchers watched the plants over a period of several days to see how they managed to get themselves securely entwined about the nearest support. They discovered that every two hours the tendrils make a 360-degree circle, reaching out and wrapping around whatever they encounter to support themselves. Not only do morning glories offer us a beautiful curtain of blue in the garden, but their diligence in seeking out what they need for support can encourage us as we seek the support we need in our lives.

5

Seeding

As you drop the seed, as you plant the sapling,
your left hand hardly knows what your right hand
is doing. But Nature knows, and in due time
the Power that sees and works in secret
will reward you openly.
—Oliver Wendell Holmes, *When We Plant a Tree*

Growing plants from seeds rather than purchasing them as nursery stock is a gardening pleasure second only to starting plants from cuttings. Nothing matches the magic of watching seedlings emerge from the ground just days after you've sown the seeds.

Although growing seedlings may not provide the immediate gratification of transplanting, it can be much more satisfying, because when we plant seeds, we're furthering a plant's purpose—reproduction. A flower is a pollinator attractor, enticing flying insects with its color, form, and fragrance so they'll carry pollen from stamen to pistil. Plant ovaries produce offspring through seeds. Sometimes all it takes for fertilization to occur is the wind. However it happens, the seeds that are produced will eventually fall to the ground and spring up as "volunteers" wherever they land—unless the gardener harvests the seeds while they're still on the plant. New plants, progeny of the parent plant, germinate and break the surface of the soil, and the whole process begins again.

Gardeners who collect, trade, and purchase seeds have a hand in perpetuating this cycle of life. Seeding also offers money-saving benefits, because growing plants from seed is cheaper than buying nursery-grown plants. And while most garden centers carry only a few varieties of a certain plant, seeds offer you many more choices. For example, I love the twenty-four-inch-tall marigolds, particularly the nearly white ones. A ninety-nine-cent packet of cream-colored marigolds will yield two dozen plants, plants you would be unlikely to find in a garden center, where the dwarf yellows and oranges are generally the only ones available.

I like big, tall zinnias, too, but nurseries rarely grow these plants for sale to the public. By the time they're in bloom, zinnias may need staking, and that's too much extra work for the nurseryman. Also, taller plants don't ship as well, so what you usually find at garden centers are plants that grow only twelve to sixteen inches tall. With seeds, however, you can grow everything from asters to zinnias, and you can choose the varieties and colors you like.

Another advantage to seeding directly into your garden is that the seedlings that emerge at germination will be acclimated to your specific growing conditions from the time they put out their first true leaves. If they don't like the conditions that exist where you've planted them, if the soil is too wet or dry or there's too much shade or sunshine, they simply won't thrive. But instead of losing a three-dollar plant, you lose a half-cent seed. The plants that do live through this emergence stage almost always turn out to be hardier than transplanted nursery stock, so although you must be patient and live through the anxiety of wondering whether or not your seeds will ever germinate, seeding is well worth the wait.

I've grown plants from seed for more than thirty years, yet I never lose my sense of wonder at the miracle of walking out one morning and seeing the first hint of green on brown as the seeds I sowed ten days earlier begin to push their way into the light. Growing plants from seeds is an exercise in faith. Even though there are always some casualties—there are times when not one seed in the packet ever germinates—each time the miracle of germination happens in my garden, my faith in the miracle of life is strengthened, and I'm spiritually renewed.

Seeding rather than buying nursery plants also gives the option of growing plants from seeds that have been saved from the previous year's crop or received from another gardener. Some gardeners are interested in growing "heirloom plants"—plants that are no longer grown commercially but that have virtues that make them both desirable and collectible. "These seeds are treasured by gardeners for providing a living link to and taste of our past. Their patchwork of antique genes, which would otherwise be lost forever, is a gift of biodiversity to the garden."[1] Some antique varieties can be shared and grown only from seed since they are not available as plants in most garden centers.

Seed packets give instructions for planting whatever type of seed they contain, but here are some general rules to follow when growing plants from seed:

1. Plant in soil that has been raked as free of rocks or gravel as possible. You want a row or patch of soil that is almost the consistency of commercial potting soil, at least in the immediate area where you're planting.
2. Make sure the soil is warm enough for germination to occur, or the seeds will just rot in the wet, cold ground.
3. "Sow dry and set wet" is an ancient adage that simply means to sow seeds in dry soil and set out plants in soil that is moist but not actually wet. Seeds are easier to han-

dle when no moisture is involved, but as soon as they're in the ground and covered, the patch or furrow should be thoroughly misted down and kept moist until the plants emerge and the roots are well established.

4. Plant seeds at a depth approximately four times their size. Tiny ones can just be pressed into the soil, but bigger ones need to be planted deeper. If there's danger of the seeds getting dried out from sun and wind, and you can't be around to water several times a day until germination, consider planting a little deeper and covering the rows with a fine layer of mulch, like straw or pine needles.

5. If you plant indoors first, be sure you have a good, direct light source, like a fluorescent grow light hanging six inches above the seedling flats. Too many new gardeners think seeds planted in cottage-cheese containers on a windowsill will do just fine, but they end up with two-inch, spindly seedlings leaning toward the window on fragile, translucent stems. Window-ledge sunlight is just not enough. This is one reason I would rather plant seeds directly in the garden as soon as the soil can be worked. If you live in a northern climate and really want to get into the "grow your own" seedling business, you should investigate the use of cold frames or small greenhouses.

6. After your seedlings emerge or after you transplant them from indoors, cover them with a tent of hay or pine needles to protect them from the brutal sun. This mulch will also help keep the soil around each seedling moist.

Staying Grounded

When we grow our plants from seeds, we make a leap of faith, but we also take control of what goes into our gardens. Those two things may seem contradictory, but they often go together.

Gardeners, even those of us who go in for the cottage or wild garden look, are interested in controlling their environment and doing it in a "mighty public way," as the stage manager in *Our Town* would say. We like to choose what we wake up to every morning—what we see, touch, smell, taste, and hear outside the walls of our houses. Some gardeners love the tinkling sound of wind chimes and have them hanging in trees and from hooks all around the yard. Others are much happier with the sounds of birds singing, squirrels barking, and wind blowing through leafy branches and don't want to introduce anything artificial to their environment. Whatever style we prefer, when we start our plants from seed, we're saying we want to have more choices and more control over what goes on in our gardens.

But to have the variety and vitality of plants that come with being a "seeder" rather than a "setter," we have to risk failure. We have to believe we can nurse our seedlings into good, strong plants that won't need our care as much once they're established. It's like raising kids, in a way. My husband, who has no biological children, says that choosing to have children is an incredible act of optimism. Folks who are grounded in the garden are optimistic too; we believe in our power to make things happen, and we love it when our plans work out. The Book of Proverbs says, "Commit your works to the LORD And your plans will be established" (Proverbs 16:3, NASB). Spiritual gardeners know that when they step out in faith and become co-creators with God, their hopes and plans are much more likely to be realized.

Finally, we can acquire a new sense of respect for the un-hurried pace of the natural world when we propagate our plants from seeds. In the Gospels of the Bible, Jesus compares the kingdom of heaven, as well as faith, to a mustard seed. In the Book of Luke we read, "Then Jesus asked, 'What is the king-dom of God like? What shall I compare it to? It is like a mustard seed, which a man took and planted in his garden. It grew and became a tree, and the birds of the air perched in its branches'" (Luke 13:18-19).

If we have the patience, we can grow trees from tiny seeds. And as the results of our patience and our labor become apparent, our faith grows as well.

Soul Gardening

In what area of your life do you need to commit to intentional seeding and patient waiting? In what ways does having faith feel out of control to you? Consider the risks of seeding and waiting and the potential gain from taking those risks. Then, as you become more grounded in your faith in God, observe the ways in which your plans come to fruition.

Hardening Off

*Young plants require a smooth transition from
their protected environment indoors to
their outdoor growing conditions.*
—Smith and Hawken, *The Book of Outdoor Gardening*

When I lived farther north where the cold, dreary days of February seemed to go on forever, I couldn't wait to see something growing in the winter—even if it was under fluorescent grow lights on my kitchen table. Gardeners who live in zones that have long winters will be interested in the idea of starting seeds under lights, in cold frames, or in greenhouses. The reward of watching tiny seedlings emerge from moist soil when the world outside your window is locked in the grip of winter makes the effort worthwhile. Growing your own plants year-round gives you something to do besides drooling over seed catalogs and planting someday-gardens in your mind as you wait for spring to return.

Whether you raise the seedlings yourself indoors or purchase them from a nursery or garden center when spring arrives, you can successfully get them into the garden without shocking them into an early death through a technique called "hardening off." This is a way of easing seedlings into the outdoors by gradually introducing them to the conditions they'll have to get used to in their permanent home, such as brighter sunlight, stronger breezes, and unpredictable temperature changes. In warmer planting zones where cold temperatures aren't an issue, the challenge is to get plants acclimated to the drying effects of sun and wind after being sheltered in a protected, well-watered environment all their young lives.

For the first two or three days, take your seedlings outside and place them in a shady, relatively warm spot for no longer than four hours. Check on them often, and don't let the sun and wind dry them out. Sometimes plants will revive after being stressed by neglect, but the resulting weakening of the plant can cause stem damage that might be fatal. When you're hardening off your plants, it's important to pay attention and to schedule it on days when you'll be around during the period you have them outside. You'll need to keep them watered and bring them back inside once their adjustment time has elapsed.

For three to seven days, increase the time your plants spend outdoors each day by about thirty minutes. As they get used to the elements, they'll grow stronger than they were when they were under lights or in the greenhouse. Their first exposure to real sunlight may be a shock to their systems, so introduce them to it gradually. When you put them out in the sun, make the first few visits brief, no more than thirty minutes.

Continue this regimen until the plants can make it through most of the day without wilting. Remember that once they're in the ground, the plant's roots will have more protection than they did in the pots, so if they're properly hardened off, you can expect good results from both your homegrown and store-bought nursery stock.

Staying Grounded

Do you ever rush headlong and headstrong into things? Do you sometimes look back and realize that in a fit of frenzy you "took the road less traveled" but, unlike poet Robert Frost, came to regret it because you were ill prepared and hadn't really thought things through? William Wordsworth wrote, "The world is too much with us, late and soon."[1] Most people would agree that these words are truer today than when he penned his poem. The world tells us to "strike while the iron is hot" and "just do it!" Think of other popular expressions you've heard throughout your life that urge you to be aggressive and make things happen for yourself:

"The early bird catches the worm."

"Time waits for no man."

"Time is money."

"Procrastination is the thief of time."

And my personal favorite:

> Gather ye rosebuds while ye may,
> Old Time is still a-flying
> And this same flower that smiles today,
> Tomorrow will be dying.[2]

I like the idea of hardening off, of taking time to adjust to new situations rather than jumping into them unprepared. The patience required to take tender plants outdoors and then back into shelter day after day until they're ready to be set in the garden is the same kind of patience required to adjust to major changes in our lives.

Life gives us many opportunities to grow, and it's hard to know which ones to go for and which ones to shy away from. Taking time to gentle ourselves into new situations is a luxury we can't always afford but a luxury we should relish whenever we can. Hardening off is really just buying time. If we make the time to listen to our hearts, to face changes by taking baby steps whenever possible instead of giant steps, we may find that our shifts and adjustments go more smoothly because we weather them from a position of gradually acquired strength.

Soul Gardening

Think about some of the major transitions in your life: leaving home for the first time, going to college, getting your first apartment, getting hired or changing jobs, marrying, moving, being transferred. As you look back, what did you do to harden off before making your move? What should you have done differently? Do you think it's better to dive in or ease in when confronted with change?

7

Daylily

Hemerocallis

The lily was created on the third day,
early in the morning
when the Almighty was especially full of good ideas.
—Michael Jefferson-Brown
The Lily: For Garden, Patio, and Display

I've given in to the inevitable: I've finally pulled up the rest of my leggy petunias and buried them deep in the compost heap. Central Florida early summer has enveloped us once again, and the glory of the spring garden is past. Pansies, ageratum, and sweet alyssum suffer in the rainless heat and humidity. They will be the next to go. Even the snapdragons—summer staples in northern climates—are looking too weary and worn to bother with. Best put them all out of their misery.

My roses are starting to decline, putting out fewer and smaller blossoms as the heat forces them to conserve their energy, and their blossoms tend to "blow" the same day they open. Even the geraniums look exhausted. What I need is something that likes high temperatures and bright sunlight, something that will show a new flower every day and will multiply underground, giving me even more color and cheer next year.

I search my favorite garden centers and look through gardening books for something colorful and hardy that might thrive in this laundry-room climate while I wait for the sunflowers, cornflowers, and zinnias I seeded a month ago to bloom. It's only early June, and we have a long way to go before cooler weather and fall gardens. What, besides cacti and succulents, loves the sun and heat of high summer?

Hibiscuses seem to thrive this time of year. They relish the heat and don't seem to mind the drought too much. But they're so flamboyant, rising high above the ground and showing off their exotic ballroom-skirt blossoms for everyone to admire. And I enjoy the crape myrtles, their lacy dancing-in-the-breeze clusters of crinkly flowers that come in so many gorgeous colors. But where I live, both of these turn into huge shrubs—even trees—so I plant them sparingly. What I want is color at my knees, not frills and flounces at my shoulders.

This summer I'll try daylilies.

Daylilies, *Hemerocallis,* and I go back a long way. The sight of orange or yellow daylilies securing a steep embankment, beautifying what might otherwise be a dismal landscape, always takes me back to my childhood and the miracle of finding flowers growing wild in unlikely places.

From 1960 to 1965 my family lived in a two-story house on a half-acre lot surrounded by woodlands and overgrown pastures. The creek at the end of our gravel road was good for tadpole-stalking in summer and ice skating in winter, and the open spaces on either side were havens for phlox, daisies, Queen Anne's lace, and daylilies—those plain, old-fashioned tangerine-colored ones, the native *Hemerocallis fulva,* sometimes called "tawny." Queen Anne's lace and lantana both looked pretty, but I hated the smell of them. Pinky lavender phlox and wild roses were sweet-smelling but too fragile to make the trip home with

41

me on my bicycle. The daylilies that I picked, though, were fragrant, stunning, and strong. Even if they got a little bit limp before I reached the house, they would recover in a vase of water. Days after other wildflowers had shriveled and fallen into tissue-paper confetti on the table around the vase, my daylilies were still blooming.

The hybrid daylilies we are able to grow today come in every color of the rainbow except pure white and true blue. Hybrids evolved from Chinese and Japanese species brought to North America by settlers emigrating from Europe in the seventeenth and eighteenth centuries. The tawny daylily, *H. fulva,* and a yellow one called lemon daylily, *H. flava,* were naturalized hundreds of years ago in many parts of North America, and these are the ones I fell in love with as a girl.

Once I spotted tawny and lemon daylilies mysteriously arranged in a rectangle in a clearing. Had a cabin been there years ago? Did someone plant these "lilies of the field" around her homestead in hopes of brightening an otherwise difficult, perhaps colorless life? Did the house burn to the ground and grasses and vines cover all evidence of its having been there, save for the flowers that still bloom year after year along what was the perimeter of the house? Did the flowers growing along the tree line at the edge of the forest migrate there on their own, or did she plant them there on purpose, adding a spot of sunlight to the dark edge of the woods?

I would make up stories about the daylily family while I sat on a stump in the clearing or hid in one of the makeshift forts I had built. I fancied myself a pioneer, too, and I was forever building these lean-tos in the woods so I would have a place of my own to go, to be alone, to read, write, dream, and wonder about the world. And no matter how crude the structure, I kept a jar of wildflowers in there with me, a bouquet that almost always included daylilies.

I used to think these flowers were called daylilies because they bloomed in the middle of the day and closed up by nightfall. But the word *Hemerocallis*, the botanical name for daylily's genus, is from two Greek words: *hemero*, meaning "for a day," and *callis*, or "beauty," therefore, "beauty for a day." Although it's true that the individual flowers last only a day, their scapes (or stems) produce clumps of buds at their tips, one of which opens as the dying one falls off, so there's a new blossom almost every day. This can go on for weeks and even in a vase, as one blossom fades and falls and a new one opens and takes its place.

In China daylilies were originally cultivated for their flavor. "The buds were eaten as a spring tonic and any extra buds were dried to be enjoyed during the winter months. Not only were daylilies tasty, they were also good for you, holding such diverse powers as the ability to relieve pain, cure kidney ailments, and lessen grief. This plant was called *hsuan t'sao*, 'the plant of forgetfulness,' and was said to cure sorrow by causing a loss of memory."[1]

"To relieve pain . . . and lessen grief." Maybe that's why I'm responding so to daylilies this summer, especially the ones I've planted in my garden. My mother's unexpected death at the end of March has dulled the color of my days. I'm grieving the loss of one of the most important people in my life—my friend, my love—and I'm lonely for the sunlight she shone on me so easily. Perhaps I should make a tonic of daylily buds "to relieve pain . . . and lessen grief."

Some days I miss her almost more than I can bear, yet I wouldn't wish her back from where she is now. Whenever I feel sad about her being gone, I visualize her with her two sisters and their girlfriends, all of them dressed to the nines, sitting around a table and listening to the sounds of Lawrence Welk at a heavenly USO dance. Mother is getting to know the movie stars she idolized all her life. She never tired of the far-fetched world depicted in the movies of the 1940s, where the women were all beautiful and gorgeously dressed and where the handsome men knew how to treat them like ladies. She barely separated the actors from the characters they portrayed. She loved them for creating a fantasy world where life was lovely and she could always expect a happy ending.

Maybe, when we get to heaven, we get to have the world we always wished for. If that's true, Phyllis Rose is singing with Bing Crosby, "Heaven, I'm in heaven, and my heart beats so that I can hardly speak." She is whirling around on the dance floor with Fred Astaire, dancing like Ginger Rogers, wearing a golden gown with a full skirt that's shaped—I can't help but notice—like the fully opened blossom of the hopeful, healing daylily.

Composting

Behold this compost! Behold it well! . . .
What chemistry! . . . Earth . . . grows such
sweet things out of such corruptions.
—Walt Whitman, "This Compost"

There are few more satisfying garden activities than sliding a shovel into a pile of crumbly brown compost and applying that loamy, magical material to a newly cleared garden patch or using it to side-dress a shrub, a garden row, or a tree. Compost is a gift from you and nature to your plants, an invaluable addition to the soil and the primary building material of all good gardens.

And it's free.

Unlike those forty-pound bags of "compost" available for sale at the garden supply store, what I'm talking about is the kind you make yourself the old-fashioned way. You take all the organic materials from your kitchen, garden, and lawn, pile them together, and just let the pile rot. The theory behind organic gardening is that if you emulate nature to create the healthiest soil you can, avoiding the use of chemicals as much as possible, your plants will withstand occasional attacks of insects, fungus, and weeds, because they'll be stronger and more disease-resistant. Compost is at the foundation of all organic-gardening practices.

For anywhere from a few months to more than a year, depending on weather conditions and the energy and materials I put into my compost piles, I feed them the leftovers of my house and garden. I layer shredded newspaper with kitchen wastes, grass clippings, garden soil, and, when I take the time to get it, well-rotted horse manure from a nearby stable. It's not wise to use pet manure; it's nasty stuff and takes a long time to break down. I turn my compost heap with a pitchfork occasionally and water it down with a hose or sprinkler during dry spells. I pick up five-pound bags of used coffee grounds for free at the local coffee shop and sprinkle them over the pile. Earthworms seem to know where the pickings are good as they migrate into my compost piles on their own, consuming the raw materials and speeding up the decomposition process. Earthworm castings—the waste product they leave behind as they literally eat their way through detritus—are some of the richest materials you can put on a garden. Earthworms and the heat generated by decomposition of all this organic material transform it into a priceless soil builder—completely on the house.

Composting satisfies the need gardeners have to be good stewards of the earth, to be part of the solution in caring for our natural resources rather than the problem. Every time something goes into the compost pile, it's being recycled into material that will improve the soil; that same material thrown in a garbage bag or put down the disposal will ultimately cause waste-management problems for your community. Choosing to compost is about choosing the person you really want to be: a producer rather than merely a consumer.

Composting is also the clearest illustration I know of nature's affinity for redemption and regeneration, because it transforms waste material into a medium teeming with life-giving organisms. What you see in that shovel as you fill your wheelbarrow is rich, nourishing, soil-building humus. Burned toast and spent tea bags, rotten fruit left too long in the bowl on the table, those crispy alyssum plants that died in the drought—all our culinary mistakes and horticultural missed opportunities are converted into something elemental, revitalizing, and restorative.

Like most gardening disciplines, composting is a human endeavor that attempts to imitate what nature does spontaneously to keep the life cycle cycling. Fields and forests alike provide models for gardeners to follow. Over the course of time, dead leaves and lichens, moss and molds, insect bodies and animal droppings devolve into the rich humus that gives the forest its fertility. You know that earthy smell of decomposing leaves that rises up to meet you as you shuffle along woodsy trails? That's the scent of compost.

This process of using nature's way of decomposition and regeneration to grow food has been going on for centuries. Societies that incorporated composting into their agricultural practices thousands of years ago were able to grow a great deal of food on very little land, thus supporting large populations that still thrive today. The Chinese, whose huge populations have always been supported by careful farming practices, including composting, are a case in point. Civilizations that ignored the process did so at their peril and to the demise of their cultures.

I reside in a small city on the outskirts of Orlando known for its stately homes on tree-lined brick streets. Most of my wealthier neighbors have impeccably groomed yards that are maintained by weekly crews of landscapers who don't spare chemical fertilizers, herbicides, and insecticides. I never see the homeowners outside working in their gardens, and, in fact, what passes for gardens in these yards is perfectly manicured but uninspired landscaping. I don't place my three compost piles out in the front yard for all to see, but I'm often asked what kind of mulch I use around the base of all my plants. When I tell people I make my own compost, they're amazed that such a sixties thing could be going on in the heart of a city like Winter Park.

My wild cottage garden with its blanket of compost, alive with earthworms, may be an anomaly in my neighborhood, but I believe in gardening as organically as possible, both in how I design and in what I put into my gardens, so naturally I make compost. Earth-conscious gardeners, even if they resort to an occasional shot of chemical fertilizer or a cautious spray of insecticide when some bug is taking over a whole section of the garden, are not only going to have a healthier landscape but are working to make this a better world.

Staying Grounded

Composting is the best illustration I know of the concept of grace. Grace is the gift from God that takes the messes we make, the garbage we create through careless living, the opportunities we let pass by, and the time we waste and turns them into something positive and growth-producing. Grace is a second chance, an offer of forgiveness, and an opportunity to transform the errors and shortcomings of our past into spiritual nourishment for the future.

None of us gets it right all the time. How often have we said or done something we wish we hadn't? How much energy do we spend regretting that wasted time or neglected opportunity? Grace invites us to put aside remorse and move on. Grace allows us to forgive ourselves, and it transforms our mistakes into opportunities for spiritual growth.

Each day as I take out the scraps from my kitchen, I visualize that pile of garbage as dark, rich loam. Each time I help my neighbor empty the grass clippings from his mower bag onto my compost heap, I think of the nitrogen those clippings are adding to the mix. Each time I bring home grounds from Starbucks for the garden, I make my offering to the compost pile and count it as grace. The life-giving humus these castoffs will become I count as blessing.

Like so many gardening tasks, composting is an act of faith. It takes faith to believe that what most folks put down the garbage disposals or out on the curb in black plastic bags will someday be feeding our roses. It takes faith to believe that the difficult times, the mistakes, the sins of our lives can be part of our spiritual growth. The Book of James encourages us to "Consider it pure joy . . . whenever you face trials of many kinds, because you know that the testing of your faith develops perseverance. Perseverance must finish its work so that you may be mature and complete, not lacking anything" (James 1:2-4).

Dealing with the residue of our mistakes and missteps can be discouraging. Believing that "trials of many kinds" can test our faith, develop perseverance, and grow us into mature, spiritually alive people can give us the hope we need to get through these ordeals. We would do well to remember that, like the cast-off leavings from the kitchen and yard that are transformed into rich, life-giving humus, the mistakes and missteps of our lives can be used by God to transform us into spiritually mature, fully developed people, "not lacking anything."

Soul Gardening

How can you use what seems like the "manure" of your past to create a more life-affirming atmosphere in your home or workplace today?

Write or talk about a mistake or bad decision you made, one from which you thought you might never recover. As you look back now, how did that experience become a part of who you are today? What kind of trials or temptations are you struggling with right now? Can you figuratively toss these into the compost pile and turn them over to God so He can transform them into energy for you? Pray for the faith to believe that the difficulties of today will bring new life tomorrow.

9

Fertilizing

*The longer I live the greater is my respect
for manure in all its forms.*
—Elizabeth von Arnim, *Elizabeth and Her German Garden*

When the nutritional needs of your plants outstrip what even compost-rich soil can provide, it's time to augment your soil with some kind of fertilizer. Most commercial fertilizers contain a combination of nitrogen (N), phosphorus (P), and potassium (K). The three numbers on the bags or boxes of fertilizer indicate the percentage of N-P-K in the mix. A mixture that encourages lots of green growth will have a higher nitrogen number; one that stimulates blooming will contain more phosphorus. Potassium is needed for strong root systems. You have to choose the fertilizer you put onto your garden according to each plant's specific needs.

For example, I side-dress my roses and other plants whose main feature is their blossoms with a "bloom booster" that has a high P number, but I avoid using the same fertilizer on my caladiums and coleus plants, which I grow for the leaves, not the blossoms. When I'm raising lettuce or collards, I don't want them to bloom, so I use a high-nitrogen fertilizer. I use something like kelp meal, which is high in potassium, when I side-dress caladiums, lilies, beets, and carrots—all root crops.

Fertilizers come in two categories: natural and synthetic. Natural fertilizers include but are not limited to products such as bone meal (2-14-0.2 in N-P-K percentages); blood meal (15-1.3-0.7); fish emulsion or fish meal (4-4-1); eggshells (1.2-0.4-.01); Epsom salts, coffee grounds, and limestone (not rated for N-P-K); kelp meal (1-0.5-2.5); and soybean meal (7-0.5-2.3). These products are available at most garden supply stores, in pharmacy departments (Epsom salts), or right in your kitchen (eggshells and coffee grounds). Natural fertilizers are not nearly as powerful as synthetic fertilizers, many of which have N-P-K numbers in the double digits. The advantage of natural fertilizers is that they physically become a part of your soil, so they not only feed your plants but also contribute to your efforts to build up the structure of your soil. Liquid and granular synthetic fertilizers dissolve into the soil (and, unfortunately, run off into our streams and lakes) rather than becoming a part of the soil itself.

A goal of all good gardeners should be to do no harm. But plants need nutrients to live, and it's quite difficult, although not impossible, to keep from giving in to the miracles of modern chemistry and using synthetic fertilizers at times. Our intent should be to use organic or natural fertilizers as much as we can, and when we have to resort to the convenience and availability of chemically produced fertilizers, to use them sparingly and responsibly. Moderation in our use of commercial fertilizers is the key to keeping our plants growing healthy and strong while keeping our waterways clean and free of chemical runoff.

Many novice gardeners believe that if a little fertilizer is good, a lot is even better, but too much fertilizer can kill the very plants you're trying to feed. This is called "burning" a plant and can happen whether you're using commercial fertilizers or animal manure. How well I remember my first foray into a chicken house to shovel a truckload of manure for one of my early gardens in Arkansas. I intended to put it all in my compost pile, because I had been warned that chicken manure was very "hot" and would burn my plants unless it had time to cure properly. But I had so much of the stuff that I decided to side-dress my tomato and okra plants with just a little of it. Three days later, all those plants were brown and crisp from too much nitrogen.

As I said earlier, nitrogen makes plants leafy and green, but too much of it can also encourage rapid growth that causes plants to become tall, spindly, and weak. If you're growing plants for their flowers or their fruits, which includes all vegetables, too much nitrogen will delay blooming and fruiting. What you'll end up with, for example, are huge, leafy eggplant bushes that never bloom and produce eggplants.

On the other hand, phosphorus stimulates plants to bloom, but too much phosphorus is an environmental hazard. Excess nitrogen and phosphorus escape our lawns and gardens as runoff and eventually flow into streams and lakes, stimulating an overproduction of algae. These algae demand oxygen to live, and they use up all the oxygen that naturally occurring organisms in the lake or stream need to survive. As it continues to grow and spread, the algae bloom cuts off sunlight, killing plants that are trying to survive below. The decomposition of these dead plants, which would have been food to fish and other wildlife, causes the water to darken and smell bad. Fish begin to die, contributing to the degradation of the lake or stream. This is why it's imperative that we learn to use fertilizers wisely and not contribute to this problem.

Using plant and animal manures has the advantage of adding "roughage" to your soil, but it doesn't eliminate the excess runoff problem. If you live near or on a body of water, your wise and frugal use of all kinds of fertilizers is a responsibility you can't afford to ignore. As gardeners, we're tenders of the earth, and we should treat the earth tenderly. Educate yourself about all the ways you can keep your gardens flourishing without causing harmful organisms in the water to flourish as well.

The ancient Greeks had two sayings carved above the doorway to the oracle at Delphi's shrine: "Know Thyself" and "Nothing in Excess." We can use similar rules for fertilizing our gardens: "Know Thy Plants and Thy Fertilizers" and "Nothing in Excess."

Staying Grounded

Building up our gardens with healthy, organic additives rather than chemical quick-fix fertilizers is like building our bodies by eating foods that contribute to our health rather than those that give us a momentary sugar or fat high, which ultimately impairs our physical health. Similarly, if we build up the soil of our souls by finding meaning and joy in developing ourselves as spiritual beings and by feeding our souls a healthy diet of spiritual food, we won't need the artificial stimulants our culture offers us as ways to escape reality.

By creating sustainable organic gardens, we can minimize our need for the synthetic chemicals that give our plants a quick boost of energy but degrade our ecosystem. By working to create balance and harmony in our lives, we can find happiness in ways that don't require food or other artificial mood-enhancers. When we feed our souls spiritual truth, we're more likely to maintain a sense of purpose, and our living environment—our families, our jobs, our friendships—remain unpolluted.

Soul Gardening

Name one thing you should give up or severely limit in your life—something you're using, doing, or thinking about in excess that's not good for you or your environment. Ask God to release you from this habit's power and to take it away. If you need help, seek the counsel of one or two people you trust.

10

Nap-at-Noon
Ornithogalum umbellatum

There is not a flower that opens,
not a seed that falls into the ground,
and not an ear of wheat that nods on the end of its stalk
in the wind that does not preach and proclaim
the greatness and mercy of God to the whole world.
—Thomas Merton, *The Seven Storey Mountain*

All plants have botanical names that classify them according to their common characteristics into genera and species. With the unwieldy botanical name *Ornithogalum umbellatum,* one particular plant, not surprisingly, has come to be known by several common names, including "star-of-Bethlehem," "summer snowflake," and "nap-at-noon." The first two names refer to the plant's six-petaled blossoms. The last one refers to the plant's tendency to close up those white blossoms around the middle of the day. I prefer "nap-at-noon" or "noon-flower," because they describe how the plant behaves rather than how it looks. I also respond to this name because, like the plant, I tend to fade and close up sometime around the middle of the day. I like a plant with which I can identify.

Most afternoons, unless something extraordinary prevents me, I lie down to "rest my eyes" just long enough to get past the sleepiness of a day that began around five o'clock and has gone nonstop ever since. This noontime ritual is both nurturing and regenerating. It's something I do for myself, although my husband and son will tell you that the happier, more rested person who arises from these *siestas* is a gift to them as well. Like a hot, fragrant bath or a good book and a cup of tea on a rainy afternoon, a nap is a celebration of relaxation, a gift to the body and the spirit.

I have the uncanny ability to decide how long I want to sleep—whether ten minutes or thirty—check my watch, fall asleep, and wake up at whatever time I designated. I dive down into slumber and resurface twenty or thirty minutes later, shaking off the lassitude that naturally follows a midday snooze.

What usually brings me back to consciousness is remembering what I ought to be doing: all those responsible, grownup things I do to feel productive. Sometimes the line between resting and deep sleep is so thin that I know I slept at all only by a metallic taste on my tongue, as though I had been sucking on a silver spoon. I may not have been born with one in my mouth, but my noontime naps do give me a taste of luxuriousness. Those who can afford a nap at noon are wealthy indeed.

I know I shouldn't feel guilty when I open my eyes with spoon-mouth and fog-brain, but I do. I wasn't raised to feel ashamed of taking afternoon naps. In fact, I grew up in a family that accepted the nap at noon as one of society's civilizing influences. Like early to bed and early to rise, an apple a day, and attending church on Sundays, napping, we were taught, was part of living wisely and well.

On sultry summer days in the early 1950s with the heavy air stirred only by a wire-caged window fan, my mother sometimes left my sister and me at my grandmother's house in Louisville while she ran her errands. My grandmother—"Mother Hill," as she requested we call her—lived in the West End, the old part of the city embraced by the crook of the Ohio River where it elbows around the top peak of the state of Kentucky. In the morning before the sun was too high, we often walked with Mother Hill to the Kroger, and even early in the day it was a long, hot walk down Market Street for us little girls. Mother Hill let us take turns pulling her two-wheeled, metal shopping cart up over the granite curbs and along the cracked and buckled sidewalks. Ancient maples lined the streets, and over the years their resolute roots had corrugated the concrete as their friendly boughs shaded the walkway.

"Walk fast in the sun and slow in the shade," Mother Hill advised us. The smell of cooking asphalt rose to meet us as we hurried over the sunny spots and poked along under the leafy canopy on our way to and from the grocery store.

Back at her home, Mother Hill heated Campbell's tomato soup and made grilled cheese sandwiches for lunch, and we had better eat it all, or the frown lines between her eyebrows gathered into a disapproving scowl. If we cleaned our plates, though, for dessert we would get windmill cookies, those spicy, gingery treats shaped like windmills that tasted better with lemonade than anything else.

After lunch we would all go down for our naps, although my sister and I were never tired and always hated spending an hour of the afternoon so foolishly. First we had to wash up in the green-tiled bathroom that smelled of Palmolive soap. Then we would lie down on one of the three beds in Mother Hill's room or on the double bed in the back room.

Lying in Mother Hill's bedroom, trying hard as I could to keep from falling asleep, I would think about how my mother had slept in the same daybed when she was my age. I wondered what growing up in that house had been like. Three girls and two parents had shared a two-bedroom, one-bath house until all three girls were married. Even as a child, I knew those had to be close quarters.

Sometimes as I lay there, I would hear the strawberry man going down the street in front of the house with his horse clip-clopping, its harness jingling, and him singing, "STRAWWW-berries! Get your nice red STRAWWWWberries!"

Or I would hear the truck gardener, a man from the country who sold his produce at Mother Hill's doorstep, weighing out onions, potatoes, apples, or peaches—whatever was in season—on a big metal scale that hung on the side of the truck.

Other times I heard the clinking sound of the ragman's cart in the alley behind the house. "Rags . . . bottles . . . old iron," he sang out. My mother told me that when she was a little girl, she and her sisters thought he was chanting, "Rags . . . bottles . . . ALARM!" and they would hide under the bed as he passed.

On the very best summer afternoons, the fragrance of freshly baked cookies, pies, rolls, and loaves of bread wafted through the open window as the "Donaldson man" from Donaldson's Bakery moved slowly down the street. How clever of him to open the bread drawer on his truck from time to time. The yeasty smell announced his arrival and served as his silent but effective calling card. These were the sounds and smells that lulled me into my naps at noon as a little girl.

When I opened my eyes with the taste of nap in my mouth and Mother Hill smelling of Palmolive soap and her afternoon bath, wearing a fresh housedress and leaning over me, she was singing, "Lazy Mary, will you get up, will you get up, will you get up?" There would be my pretty young mother, back from her errands, singing right along with Mother Hill as though she knew this was the way life was supposed to be: the daily trip to Kroger, the walking fast in the sun and slow in the shade, windmill cookies and lemonade, the song of the strawberry man fading in the distance, and the gracious, kindly ritual of the afternoon nap.

11

Heeling In

Patience and tenacity of purpose are worth more
than twice their weight of cleverness.
—Thomas Henry Huxley
The Collected Essays of Thomas Henry Huxley

At the end of our first meeting about collaborating on an article for a gardening magazine, my new friend Michele sent me on my way with a five-gallon bucket of freshly cut roses from her garden, three dozen of them at least. I buried my face in the blossoms and sank into their perfume at the first traffic light I came to. *This,* I thought, *is heaven.* Cut flowers from a friend's garden are an utter blessing. They require nothing but a vase of water to brighten an entire room or, in my case, an entire Honda CR-V.

Several weeks later, Michele brought over a dozen bare-root stock, experimental rose bushes that she had been given to test in her garden, and she offered to share them with me. I was delighted at this unexpected windfall; the only problem was that I didn't have a bed ready to put them in. You can't just stick twelve rose bushes into buckets of water without worrying about root rot. What to do?

Sometimes we're caught off guard by an unexpected gift of new planting material—a couple of extra blueberry bushes a neighbor doesn't have space for, a pot of sunflower seedlings, a rooted cutting from a friend's hydrangea bush, a dozen daylilies—and we just aren't prepared to set them out into the landscape. Yet what should you do when you don't have time to prepare the soil properly before the plants either dry up or rot? Do you want to plant them just anywhere and let them start establishing themselves, only to go through another transplant shock when you finally decide where you really want them to go? The way out of this dilemma is a simple technique called "heeling in."

Heeling in lets you put your plants on hold until you're ready to plant them. It involves digging a trench in a somewhat protected area of the yard or garden, making one side of the ditch vertical and the other a forty-five-degree angle. Each plant is laid in against the sloped side of the trench with its roots slightly below the soil level. Then the trench is filled in, and a layer of mulch is put over it followed by thorough watering. If the trench is kept moist, the plants can be left there and heeled in until the time you can say, "Ah, yes! That's where this plant is meant to be, and I finally have time to put it there."

Heeling in is a perfect solution to the problem of what to do when a friend gives you a desirable plant at an inconvenient time, when you can't do anything except receive it graciously, wondering privately, "Where in the world am I going to put *this?*" The answer is "I'm going to heel it in until I figure out where it really belongs." Heeling in allows us to be gracious, but more importantly, it buys us time.

Staying Grounded

One of the hardest things for me to do is to "heel in" and wait for the right timing before plunging into a new challenge, be it one I desire or one I dread. It's been said that gardeners have a great need to control things, and gardening is a great outlet for satisfying that desire. Let's not call ourselves control freaks—let's just say we have control issues. I believe that our compulsion to order our little horticultural worlds is reflected in our approach to other areas of our lives as well.

Just as in the garden, unexpected things come our way in life, and often we're not ready for them. We try to believe that if we just hang on, this unexpected shifting of our world will be for a good reason, but the timing seems wrong when it occurs. Maybe it's a new job or assignment, or it could be a layoff we aren't expecting. It might be the start of a new relationship, or maybe it's the end of an old one. Or, as with many baby boomers these days, it may be the call to become the caregiver to an aging and unexpectedly dependent parent.

I've recently found myself the only one of the four children in my family who is in a position to deal with my father, who has Alzheimer's disease. He is only seventy-nine, but he's suddenly become a disabled old man. Dad always believed—and the rest of the family always hoped—that he would keep working and thinking and interacting with the world until one day when he would wake up in heaven, not knowing what hit him. What has hit him is helplessness, and this is one thing he has no clue how to handle. His desire to be independent drew him away from our family for at least two decades, and now he finds himself dependent upon the kindness of virtual strangers in his life: his family—and, in particular, me.

What I have on my hands, without warning or preparation, is not a rose garden but a thorny situation. I feel pressed to make decisions about where Dad should live, how much I should be a part of his life, what my responsibilities are beyond making sure he's properly cared for, how to manage his financial assets, and how to ensure that he's not left feeling alone. Dad was always doggedly independent and basically felt that his obligations as a parent were over as soon as his kids graduated from high school.

Eventually he left my mother as well. What are my responsibilities as his daughter, considering how long it's been since he was a part of my life?

I didn't see this coming. And because I'm so new at it, I'm having trouble controlling the stress this is creating in my usually placid life. I'm fortunate to have wise people around me who know what truth looks like and are willing to give me sound advice whether I want it or not. Their advice often doesn't seem valid, because it doesn't match what my mind and emotions are telling me. *My* truth—hollow idol that it is—leans on my believing that I have to apply action and purpose to any problem I come up against. My wise counselors advise me to allow things to unfold and reveal themselves in their own time rather than to try so hard to hurry events along in order to end the anxiety of not knowing.

They tell me, in other words, to heel in and hold back until the right time and place for action present themselves. Heeling in means parking something—including my need to understand and control a situation—in a place that's not its final home and waiting for God to reveal the best time and place for it to settle. Heeling in requires faith and letting go; it requires the ability to relinquish control.

As I try to park my need for resolution and keep its roots moist until I know where to plant it, I'm being challenged to realize that even when I do find "the solution," it may be only temporary. I often heel in a plant for a few weeks and then set it out somewhere that seems suitable, only to realize months later that it was not the right spot at all. Heeling in isn't about finding a permanent place for the plant—or my problems—on the very first try. It's about not doing the first thing that comes to mind just because something new has come into my life. I'm learning that problems are usually best handled through creative problem-solving, where there's a gestation period—a time to generate ideas and then let them germinate.

One way I practice horticultural heeling in is to look for signs as to where a plant should be situated. I watch for where the early and late sunshine falls, for example, and heed the condition of the soil—where it dries out quickly, where it stays moist. I need to look for similar signs in my life that tell me what's healthiest for me emotionally, physically, and relationally—what brings me life. Life is hard going under the best of circumstances, but I'm learning to step back and observe, to listen, to pray, and then to wait in expectation for the answer to that prayer.

Giving up control, protecting what's vital, and walking in faith are what heeling in is all about. To abandon control and to have the courage and faith to wait—sometimes that's the hardest thing of all to do.

Soul Gardening

Think of times of change when, had you waited awhile and thought things through, you might have responded in a different way. What's one area of your life right now that you want to jump in and fix things either for yourself or other people? The next time you're tempted to act on your first impulse, try to stop and just breathe. Make a list of ways an immediate reaction may not serve you or others well. Learn to practice the art of heeling in.

12

Thinning

Our life is frittered away by detail. . . .
Simplify, simplify.
—Henry David Thoreau, *Walden*

If we could be sure that every seed we sow would germinate and grow, it would make sense to plant the seeds at predetermined intervals so they would be properly placed according to their space requirements, and we would not have to thin them out later. Plants that require twelve inches of space all around would be seeded twelve inches apart from one another, those that need only six inches of space would be seeded at six-inch intervals, and so on.

But since no such guarantee exists, it makes better sense to scatter more seeds than needed, fairly close together, and to thin the plants to the proper spacing after they've germinated and become established. Once they've emerged from the soil, we can select the hardiest and best-situated plants and remove the others. Then the most likely survivors will have the space they need to grow without competition from weaker neighbors.

Thinning is the process of removing excess seedlings so that those remaining have enough room to spread out and develop fully. When you grow plants by sowing directly into the garden, no matter how carefully you position the seeds at sowing time, some plants will come up too close together. This can actually aid in germination, because bunches of seeds shouldering their way through the soil together make it easier for all to emerge. They tend to shade the ground at one another's feet, helping the soil stay moist as they begin the long journey to maturity. If allowed to continue to grow right next to their neighbors, however, none of the plants will prosper. That's where thinning comes in.

Thinning can be hard for the novice gardener. Ripping perfectly good plants from the soil goes against all that we're about as caregivers of the earth. But it has to be done, or we'll end up with an overcrowded row of gangly, unproductive plants fighting for the nutrients, water, space, and sunlight they need to survive and grow.

It helps to know that we can use some of the plants we remove at thinning time as baby greens in salads and stir-fries. Think of what we pay for spring greens in the produce aisle of the supermarket. Thinning actually becomes a harvest when tender young greens like lettuce, spinach, Swiss chard, and beet tops go directly from the garden into a meal. We can also transplant some of the hardier vegetable and flower plants into other parts of the garden, as you'll see in a future chapter on transplanting. The worst thing that can happen is that the plants we pull will end up in the compost pile, where they'll add nitrogen and bulk to the mix. The conscious gardener finds ways to use everything in the garden.

Before plants get too far along, decide which ones will live and which will end up as compost or salad fixings. Choose the biggest and healthiest-looking ones, and, if possible, ones that are already positioned properly. Do this as soon as the first true leaves appear. If you wait too long to thin, the plants you elect to keep will develop poorly. Also, as the seedlings get bigger, thinning will become more difficult, because you'll have trouble not disturbing the root systems of plants you want to keep.

The late Jim Crockett wrote in his classic *Crockett's Victory Garden* that he preferred thinning his seedlings twice. After the first true leaves appeared, he thinned plants to half their final interval. When the plants grew to about two inches tall, he thinned them again to their optimal spacing.[1] I think his method has two advantages. If your seedlings undergo some attrition after your first thinning, you still have twice as many plants as you need and can use some of the extras to fill in for the dead guys. Second, once plants are two inches tall, they're big enough for you to transplant rather than uproot, so you can spread the wealth rather than just pull up the excess.

Thinning is easiest after a good rain while the soil is still moist but not soggy. Use one hand to anchor the soil around the plant you're saving, and with the other hand gently remove the unwanted plants around it. Tug at each plant you're thinning out until you can feel its roots give way. This ensures a clean removal with minimum disturbance to the plants that are to remain. Press any disturbed soil back around the plants left standing. Then water gently but deeply to settle the roots and fill in any air pockets around them. Mulch the row at this point, since without their old neighbors shading the ground around them, the remaining plants and the soil they're standing in are likely to dry out faster.

Staying Grounded

Whenever we hear the word *thinning,* most of us think about shedding excess pounds, although my husband would argue that his first thoughts run to his hairline rather than his waistline! As for me, when I thin out a row of seedlings in my garden, I tend to think about de-cluttering, not dieting.

Before we can start organizing our lives, experts tell us we have to start off-loading the stuff we don't need, the stuff that eats up our limited time, energy, space, and money without giving us a corresponding degree of enjoyment or usefulness in return. One of the fastest-growing industries in the United States right now is the personal-storage-unit business. How much of the stuff in those compartments do you think the owners ever take out, use, and enjoy in a year of paying an average of eighty dollars per month for that unit?

Thinning out our lives involves the same kind of choices we have to make when thinning the garden. What is worth keeping and what needs to go? How do I get rid of things without feeling wasteful? How do I convince myself that the things I decide to keep will look better, mean more, and be more valuable to me if they aren't hemmed in by so many things I don't need or don't really like anymore?

Take, for example, the study where I write. Everywhere I look there are stacks of papers that need to be sorted and put into some kind of file, circular or otherwise. When I want to do what is important—to write—I'm continually distracted by these piles and what they represent: my need to get order and clarity in my life. My creative energy is constricted by the sense of being surrounded by unfinished business, which distracts me from focusing on the most important things.

Thinning out our lives is therapeutic. It's an energy-yielding process, but it takes energy to make it happen. Just like the process of thinning seedlings in a garden, it also takes courage and know-how.

To begin with, we have to learn how to avoid excessive sentimental attachment to possessions. Attachment to our possessions works against our desire to de-clutter; our possessions end up possessing us rather than the other way around. Jesus warns us in the book of Matthew, "Do not store up for yourselves treasures on earth, where moth and rust destroy, and where thieves break in and steal. But store up for yourselves treasures in heaven. . . . For where your treasure is, there your heart will be also" (Matthew 6:19-21). If we're always distracted by the need to create order from the chaos in our lives, we won't be able to get to the things that are closest to our hearts. Thinning out our possessions allows us to put space around the parts of life that need room to grow.

Here's a simple plan for thinning out your home and simplifying your life. Start by choosing one closet, dresser, or room. Acquire a good supply of sturdy boxes and label them something like this: TRASH, CHARITY, RECYCLE, SELL, TBA. You may need more than one box for each category. Choose boxes that are small enough for you to lift after you fill them.

Now remove *everything* from the area you are tackling. By completely emptying that closet or drawer, you'll be able to see exactly what you have. Clean the drawer, closet, or cabinet thoroughly. Seeing that clear, clean space will motivate you to return only the truly important things and to put the rest in one of your five boxes.

1. *Trash.* Discard anything that's broken, beyond repair, or has missing parts; is beyond its expiration date; is one of many of the same item, such as old toothbrushes, paper clips, hangers; or is paperwork more than five years old except for important lifetime documents.

2. *Charity.* After my mother died and I had to go through her belongings, I discovered that if I put her usable belongings into a box labeled "Charity," I felt good. "Goodwill" or "Salvation Army" wouldn't have had the same effect. Thinking of someone else using her gently worn items made it easier for me to part with things that still held memories for me. I now apply the charity label when giving away my own unnecessaries, and that label makes it much easier to part with them. One more thing: put items that someone else might be able to use on the curb

next to your garbage cans on trash pickup day where people who may need them will see them and help themselves. Remember the old saying about one person's trash being another person's treasure. I once got a baby bed in perfect condition this way!

3. *Recycle.* Put old newspapers, magazines, bottles, plastic or paper bags, jars, and cans into the recycle box. Take them to the proper bins or the recycling center, or put them on the curb on recycling day. You can recycle those arts-and-crafts supplies you've been meaning to use for twenty years by donating them to your local school's art department or to a retirement home.

4. *Sell.* If you have trouble parting with your things because you spent a lot of money on them, you might feel better if you have a yard sale, take them to a consignment shop, or sell them in an online auction or through an ad in the paper. Turning trash into treasure is rewarding, but for me it's too much trouble for the little bit of money involved.

5. *TBA* (to be assigned). At this point you'll still have items you aren't sure what to do with. Put these things in the TBA box to go through later. Then put an "expiration date" on the side of the box. After that date, everything in it will go to charity unless you've decided why you're keeping it and where you'll put it. If you still can't decide by the expiration date, those items are history.

Now gather up these boxes and take them to the appropriate places. You can figure that part out on your own; gardeners are problem-solvers. The important thing is to get them off your property. Otherwise, you may be tempted to drag some of the stuff back into your life.

When we take stock of what we have and thin out our possessions to what we really want, need, and use, we create a healthier environment for our spirits to grow in. Just like our gardens, our spirits will prosper when we create spaces within our lives by thinning out what's not important and paying attention to what is.

Soul Gardening

Take time today to follow these instructions and to thin out one area of your life—even if all you can manage is one drawer, one shelf in a closet, or one pile of papers from your to-do basket. Just do it! Give yourself credit for your accomplishment, and reward yourself in some way for taking one small step toward living a less cluttered life.

13

Sunflower

Helianthus annuus

The annual Helianthus *or sunflower towers like a priest*
raising the monstrance over the lesser folk in prayer
and strives to resemble the orb which he adores.
—Maurice Maeterlinck, *Old-fashioned Flowers*

Last Saturday at our local farmers' market, Earl Wilson's nursery stand had sold out of potted sunflowers by eight o'clock that morning. The full-blooming plants he was offering might stay in flower another week or so in the garden before the single-flower heads start turning to seed and declining. Since these are a "dwarf mammoth" variety—an oxymoron if there ever was one—they aren't repeat bloomers, so once they start going to seed, the plant is finished in terms of floral interest. I watched in amazement as customers carried them off by the box loads at three bucks a pop. Mammoth varieties produce just one huge head, and that's it; once the flower head loses its outer petals, and the individual florets in the corolla start turning to seed, these big boys quickly devolve into unattractive, raggedy brown stalks. That's why they're often relegated to the back of the border or to the vegetable patch.

Still, the fact that they were selling so well speaks to the resurgence of the sunflower's popularity. There's something lovable about this noble yet folksy colossus. Whether they're growing in the border or sitting in a vase, sunflowers look simply splendid. Sold as cut flowers in buckets on roadsides and in florist shops, sunflowers are as much at home in the living room as in the landscape. And since they're so easy to grow from seed, there's no reason even to think about buying them in pots for three to five dollars a plant.

I grow my vegetables, flowers, and herbs all together—good cottage gardener that I am—so I plant my sunflowers among everything else. I love to watch morning glory vines discover these stout, hairy stems and start climbing right to the top of them. I've planted pole beans around sunflowers, allowing the beans to take advantage of the support these giants can provide them. I like sunflowers in the back, front, and middle of my garden beds, and I love trying out new varieties.

Shooting up ten feet or more and towering over merely mortal plants, these golden goliaths have been the symbol of royalty, even divinity, in more than one ancient civilization. Just as the sun was worshiped in times past as a divine source of life, sunflowers must have seemed like the gods' manifestation to their people on earth. As the sun's position in the sky changes throughout the day, a sunflower will bend to face it, a consequence of the plant's need to capture as much solar energy as possible. Ancient people might easily have viewed this phototrophic behavior as an indication that the flower was a fellow worshiper of their god of life, the sun.

Not only are they outstanding in appearance and size—some flower heads get as large as eighteen to twenty-four inches across—sunflowers have also provided a source of food and oil for centuries. *Helianthus* is a North American native, the only major crop to originate in the lower forty-eight states. Sunflowers produce the world's second most important and valuable oil seed; only coconut oil is more widely produced and consumed. Their seeds contain thirty-five to forty percent oil, are high in polyunsaturated fat, and contain no cholesterol. They are a good source of protein, starch, and calories.

Some Native Americans were quite dependent on sunflower seeds, using them to make flour and oil for cooking, soap, and hair tonic. In fact, one wonders why the sunflower wasn't chosen as our national flower instead of the rose. It's native to our soil, and it has been our gift of beauty and nourishment to the rest of the world for half a millennium. The sunflower is the true "American Beauty."

The sunflower may look like one huge flower atop a thick, sturdy stem, but it's actually a composite of tubelike flowers called "disk florets" arranged on a flat disk and surrounded by a ring of flat, golden, bronze, or white, red, or orange petals called "ray florets." What appears to be the center of the flower is actually as many as two thousand individual florets, each one a complete flower that will, if pollinated, produce a single seed.

Like most flowers in the family Compositae, each floret contains both the male and female reproductive organs, so these big beauties are prolific in their seed production. This gets us back to the folks paying three dollars for what amounts to one seed's development. You want sunflowers? Toss out some seeds in the spring and then stand back. If you allow even one of those disks to go to seed at the end of its growing season, you'll not only feed the birds and squirrels through the late summer and fall, but you'll also have an amazing crop of volunteer sunflower seedlings the following spring. In warmer zones, it's not uncommon to get a second or third crop in one growing season.

Plant developers have created smaller sunflower varieties that fit into the home landscape a bit more tidily. Even though they aren't nearly as dramatic as the Mammoth varieties, these many-branching varieties produce flowers the size of *Rudbeckia* (black-eyed Susan) or giant zinnias and are repeat bloomers, so they're worth a try in the landscape. I especially love a wonderfully beautiful variety called Mexican sunflower or Tithonia, which looks like a three-foot-tall bush covered with three-inch red orange, gold-centered daises. Smaller, many-branching varieties allow the gardener to cut flowers without terminating the life cycle of the plant, and the colors these smaller varieties come in are astounding.

Still, give me a row of skyward-reaching monsters with pole beans climbing up the furry stalks. Nothing else in the plant kingdom can hold a candle to an eighteen-inch-in-diameter sunflower blossom looking down at the rest of the garden from atop a ten-foot stem.

These plants are aptly named, not only because they resemble the sun in appearance but also because they're avid sun lovers. When morning comes, sunflowers are still facing west, where the sun set the night before, but within thirty minutes of daybreak, they've turned toward the east to face the rising sun.

Like the sunflower, people are naturally drawn to the sunlight. Not only is the sun a direct source of vitamin D, but it also seems to have a positive effect on emotional and mental health. This is why, even in normally sunny climates, two or three dreary days of opaque gray skies can cause folks to feel depressed. SAD, or seasonal affective disorder, is a recognized form of depression that affects millions of people in the winter and is relieved by the arrival of spring or by light therapy. It isn't just the sun on our faces that makes us feel healthier. It's the sun shining through a windowpane as we work or relax indoors; it's knowing that the sun is out there even when we can't be. We're attracted to sunlight, to rainbows, to sun showers, sunrises, and sunsets, and research suggests that there's a connection between our physical and emotional well-being and the amount of sunlight to which we're exposed.

The sunflower offers spiritual parallels as well. In order to develop fully as people, we must turn our faces toward the sun and lean in toward God, from whom all blessings, all gifts, all good things flow. "Every good and perfect gift is from . . . the Father of the heavenly lights . . . who does not change like shifting shadows" (James 1:17). If the sun were to disappear, so would all life on earth. Without a relationship with God, a sense of connection with God, our lives lack meaning, and we can feel disconnected, purposeless, and depressed.

Irish poet Thomas Moore (1779–1852) makes the connection between love of the sun and love of one's beloved in these lines from his song "Believe Me, If All These Endearing Young Charms."

> *No, the heart that has truly loved never forgets,*
> *But as truly loves on to the close,*
> *As the sunflower turns on her God, when He sets,*
> *The same look which she turned when He rose.*[1]

For spiritual gardeners, the sunflower is both a reminder of the faithfulness of God and an example of how we should regard God, sunshine or shadow, daylight or dark: with a trust and adoration that are new every morning and that sustain us even through our darkest and coldest hours.

14

Transplanting

Gardening has the potential to make people whole again.
I want them to have that opportunity. . . .
I want my children to live in a healed world.
—Catherine Sneed
Founder of "The Garden Project" for former prisoners

I always get a bit nervous when I transplant. Even though I've been doing it for years and have learned a trick or two that keep my success rate high, it feels as though so much is at stake whenever I'm moving plants. This is especially true when I'm moving an established plant from one part of the garden to another, though transplanting from nursery pots into the garden can be tricky too. The very life of the plant is at stake. I have seen too many transplants expire from the shock of a move to take this garden task lightly.

I started a row of giant zinnias from seed about three weeks ago, and they're ready for thinning and transplanting. If I just leave them alone, they'll crowd each other, and not develop as well as they might. But it's midsummer here in the Deep South, and that can mean anything from heat waves to hurricanes—or both. Days of drought can bake the soil into stucco, literally choking the life out of newly moved plants. Sudden storms can drown transplants before they have a chance to establish themselves. So I've been waiting for the promise of cloudiness and a gentle afternoon rain to get these seedlings transplanted, but the plants are getting bigger, and I may not have the luxury of holding off for perfect meteorological conditions before I move them.

Proper transplanting allows plants to establish themselves in a new spot in the garden without putting too much stress on them. The gardener's goal is to create a welcoming and nurturing environment for each plant, thereby making the transfer as trauma-free as possible. It's inevitable that transplants will wilt, lose some lower leaves, and struggle to adjust for the first few days, but with care and attention, they'll be happier and healthier in their new home than they would have been if left in their old.

Before you start digging up a plant to move it, prepare the spot where the transplant will go. Dig a hole about twice the size of the rootball you think you'll have. You may need to dig up the plant first to see what size that is. If you do that, submerge the plant's roots in a bucket of water to protect the plant from drying out. Then prepare your hole the same way you prepared your soil for your original planting, as I talked about in chapter three on enriching the soil, mixing in a little all-purpose fertilizer, some compost, and some bone meal to strengthen the roots as they adjust to their new home.

Spread the roots of the transplant over the dirt in the bottom of the hole, and backfill with the rest of the dirt you removed from the hole. Don't bury the plant much deeper than it was at the original site unless you see roots starting to form along the bottom part of the stem as you might with zinnias, tomatoes, and marigolds. If that's happening, bury the stem deep enough to cover the new roots. This will make your plant grow even stronger than it was before.

As soon as you've covered the roots with soil, apply a layer of mulch, and water thoroughly. If you didn't add granular fertilizer when you were preparing the hole, you can water with a mild solution of liquid fertilizer, fish emulsion, or "manure tea" at this point.[1] Water your plants at least daily until they're no longer wilting in the afternoon sun. Plants moved from a shady to a sunny location will have to be watched more carefully. But don't get discouraged if you see them lying prostrate on the ground for the first day or so. With careful watering—don't drown them, but don't let the soil around them dry out—they'll be as good as new within a week or so.

Staying Grounded

Whether we're talking about people or plants, transplanting is tricky. It needs to be handled carefully. Just as in the garden, we can reduce the potential trauma of shifts and changes in our lives by applying the following gardening principles.

Prepare the soil in the new spot before you disturb the plant you're moving. Whether we're helping our adult children get out on their own or making changes in our careers or family lives, investigating the new situation as much as we can beforehand will make the transition less traumatic. Preparing the soil in our lives can mean anything from making sure we'll not be overextended financially to preparing our hearts for a new child or relationship.

Mix some of the soil from the plant's original spot with the dirt in which it's to be transplanted. As a plant spreads roots in its new location, it's nice for it to recognize some familiar soil among the new soil. Plants that have been grown in nursery pots in good potting soil with fertilizer mixed in will miss all that nutritious matter when their roots expand beyond the rootball and hit the dirt in the average garden. The trick is to mix old soil with new and to enrich the new environment so that it's as hospitable as the one the plant is accustomed to living in. Similarly, when we face transitions and changes in life, we should try not to leave everything familiar and cherished behind. Taking a bit of our "native earth" with us can make all the difference in whether we thrive or decline in our new surroundings. Holding on to some of the traditions, pleasures, values, and relationships of our previous situation will help ease us through the change.

Water thoroughly after transplanting, and look for good support. Family moves would have been much harder on me as a child had it not been for my mother's talent for connecting with others in our new community. She would find our parish church, our school, and the Knights of Columbus hall before we even made our move (preparing the soil beforehand). She got us a membership at a pool or country club in our new community to give us a place to go and a chance to make new friends. When we face changes of any kind, we need to find a community of like-minded people with whom we can enjoy camaraderie and from whom we can draw spiritual strength. This community will help "water" and support us at a time when we're weak from the change.

Soul Gardening

Think back on what it was like to leave home the first time, start your first job, have your first baby, watch your first child leave home, and so on. What other changes in your life forced you to be transplanted in some way? How did you cope with the change? What, if anything, made it easier for you?

Now think of someone who's going through a time of transplanting geographically, relationally, or spiritually. What might you do to prepare the soil, contribute extra nutrients and water, or give a little extra support until that person can make it on his or her own?

15

Mulching

*The greenness and fertility of my garden are due to vast
quantities of mulch, everything from compost to salt hay
and seaweed, and I would be happy to explain this,
enlarging on the virtues of each, if I couldn't see my
audience melting away [from boredom] on contact.*
—Eleanor Perényi, *Green Thoughts*

When you live in a climate that alternates between drought and
hurricanes, where the average temperature is somewhere in the
eighties, the average summer lasts well into October, and water
rationing is a way of life, you soon learn that your only hope for
successful gardening is to mulch. Like composting, mulching
is an idea that grew in popularity with the organic gardening
movement, although one could argue that the practice has been
around for as long as humans have been on the planet.

In medieval castles, when rushes spread on the floor of the
great hall finally became too foul for even the bath-eschewing
nobility of the day, lords and ladies would simply pack up and
move on to another castle or manor house, leaving their waste
behind them. Then the castle servants would haul out the nasty

stuff with wheelbarrows and deposit that rich, decomposing, maggot-infested material in a pile near the vegetable garden. After a season, this would have mellowed into good, old-fashioned compost, the very finest kind of mulch. These folks had no idea that they were on the cutting edge of the organic gardening movement.

Mulching is actually older than agriculture, because it's what forests do naturally—without the help of humans. If you use natural materials, mulching is a kind of on-site composting as well as a means of keeping down weeds and conserving moisture in the soil. As the wood chips, leaves, and other natural materials break down, just like detritus on forest floors, what results is humus, that rich organic matter that improves the tilth and chemical composition of the soil beneath it. I've taken a patch of sandy soil, planted annuals and perennials in it—enriching only the holes in which the plants were set—then mulched the area with several inches of shredded oak leaves, and a year later I turned over rich, brown humus where before there was only light gray sand. Mulch is the second wonder—after compost—of the gardening world.

I learned about mulching in my first garden, which was a vegetable garden. Despite all my watering, I couldn't keep the garden moist enough to survive the dry spells. Taking my cue from *Organic Gardening, Mother Earth News,* and *Crockett's Victory Garden,* I tried mulching. The hardest part was getting hold of the great quantities of mulch I needed. As a first-year teacher in 1973, I earned the great sum of $7,200 per year—barely enough to keep myself nourished and sheltered, much less to pay the per-bag prices for cypress mulch at the local gardening center. I was forced to resort to one of the things I do best: scrounging.

When neighbors raked their pine needles and put them out on the curb in black plastic bags, I would beat the garbage collectors to them and rescue that "waste" for my garden. Bags of nitrogen-rich grass clippings were the next thing I tried. (They actually worked better in the compost pile, since grass cuttings tend to mat into an impenetrable carpet unless they're mixed with other, loser material.) Later, when I moved to Arkansas, I offered to clean out barns for free to get the manure-enriched straw and hay for both my compost pile and for immediate use as mulch. I soon learned that hayseeds made for more work than the mulching saved, however. At the large public high school in Florida where I taught English, I asked the landscapers to save their bags of oak leaves for me. I would dump them in my yard, run over them with my lawn mower, and then rake the shredded leaves onto my azalea beds: free mulch.

A couple of years ago I was contemplating my need for a large quantity of mulch, enough to cover a parking area and a large azalea bed in front of my house. The forestry department in our town will deliver a load of free ground-up tree limbs, leaves, and branches upon request, but they'll bring only a full truckload, and that was about twice as much as I needed. I had just about decided to go to the garden center and start bringing home the sixty-plus bags of mulch I needed—twelve bags at a time in the trunk of my Saturn coupe—when a commercial tree-trimming truck stopped in front of the house next door. I offered to take their load of mulch off their hands, and the crew was happy to oblige. "Wish you had asked us yesterday," the head arborist said. "We'd have had a *whole* load for you then. Right now we're just finishing up, and all I can offer you is about half a load." The Lord works in mysterious ways.

Mulching around plants in the landscape not only conserves water by keeping the hot rays of the sun from directly touching the soil, but it also makes weeding much easier. Mulch keeps down weed growth, and the few weeds that do manage to grow through the mulch release their grip on the soil with a gentle tug. Mulching is also an act of beautification. We gardeners are in the business of making our little piece of Earth as attractive as possible, and a thick blanket of mulch gives the garden a finished look.

Staying Grounded

Mulching is about preserving moisture, keeping down weeds, and building up soil. As I look at my personal and spiritual growth, I want to be more mindful about how I preserve what's life-giving and allow it to sustain me. I want to eliminate as many distractions as I can from what's truly important—to keep down the weeds that sap my energy and require my time. And I want to be intentional about the life I create around me so that it builds upon itself and gives me a stronger and healthier foundation.

I also want to remember that mulching, like most garden chores, is not something I'll do once and then never have to do again. Recently my neighbor Annie, who isn't a gardener, came by and said, "So, are you all done with your mulching?" I knew what she meant: have you finished spreading out that big pile you had in your driveway last week? But even as I was finishing that mulching job, I was looking around my feet at places in the perennial bed where the mulch I had put down six months ago had washed away or had already been incorporated into the soil. So I said, "Not really. Mulch is continually breaking down into dirt, and that's good. But that also means I'm continually laying down new mulch—so I'm never really finished mulching."

A special kind of beauty reveals itself in the repetitive, the routine, and the regular. I derive a sense of comfort from the rhythm of each day, the turning of the seasons, and the assurance that this year's growth rests upon last year's work. As my mulching efforts build my garden soil from season to season, I become a part of a creative process that goes back as far as the creation of the world. When I participate in this dynamic work, I grow closer to the Creator; I recognize that my spiritual growth, too, is an organic process that sustains me as God's good work completes itself in the seasons of my life.

Soul Gardening

Name one thing that's threatening your spiritual life—a distraction, an energy-drainer, a source of discouragement. What's one way you can protect your spiritual life against that threat?

16

Four-O'clocks
Mirabilis jalapa

A garden is the mirror of a mind.
It is a place of life, a mystery of green moving
to the pulse of the year, and pressing on and
pausing the whole to its own inherent rhythms.
—Henry Beston, *Herbs and the Earth*

It's time to come in from the garden. If this were summer, I would have been indoors for hours, but it's still springtime here in Winter Park, so I can be outdoors all day if I choose.

But four o'clock marks the turning of the day for me, whatever the season. It's the time to switch gears, to get cleaned up, and to start thinking about supper and what the rest of the evening holds. Oh, I know I'll still go outside in the cool of sundown, looking for an excuse to enjoy the day fading into night—like doing a little deadheading, weeding, or watering. But the day feels more or less used up, and so am I by late afternoon, right around four o'clock.

However, for the flower named for this hour, the day is just beginning. Four-o'clocks open their sweetly scented, trumpet-shaped blossoms in the late afternoon and stay that way all night long. These perennials are the teenagers of the garden: slow to rise of a morning but up until all hours of the night. They grow fast, branch off in all kinds of unexpected directions, are gangly and awkward-looking if not groomed regularly, and are unsure of themselves until they come into their own at maturity. Easy to grow and maintain, they'll spread wherever they please and set down new roots wherever they touch ground if you don't watch and guide them. Yes, four-o'clocks are truly the adolescents of the flower garden.

Four o'clock has always been a transition time for me. When I was in elementary school, I relished throwing off my parochial-school uniform and tossing on my play clothes just about that time of day. Swinging a leg over my big-tire, one-speed bike, I would take off for an hour or so of playing with friends or just riding around by myself. Either way, four o'clock marked the transition between hours of confinement and hours of freedom, between regimentation and recreation. It was the time of day I blossomed.

But when I reached my preteen years and it was no longer cool to go out and play after school, I felt a kind of loss and loneliness at that time of day. Especially in winter, when sunlight was thin and weak and evening fell hard and fast, I felt lost and a bit bereft in the late afternoon. Maybe it was because four o'clock was the between time—not daytime anymore, but not yet evening when the day would shift to a different rhythm and pace. Being unsure of my own shifting and changing, uncertain of how the pace and tempo, volume and rhythm of my own life should go, I often sank into an ennui that lasted into the dinner hour.

Whether we like it or not—and I did *not*—"change" is the active verb in what we're about as adolescents. Yet I hated change with all my being when I was on the cusp of becoming a young woman. None of my bodily changes were going that well, at least not according to *Seventeen* magazine, and when my parents announced at the end of my freshman year in high school that we would be moving to Florida from Indianapolis, I was devastated. I had finally begun to consider myself one arc in a circle of friends at Bishop Chatard Catholic High School. I played an old, silver saxophone in my brand-new school's brand-new band, and I had learned not to go up the down stair-cases while nuns guarded the landings with their detention pads tucked into the folds of their long, black habits. I had spent five afternoons in detention one semester for being caught chewing gum on campus, so I didn't have a flawless record at Chatard, but I knew the rules and what to expect, and I guess I liked that the consequences for misbehavior were predictable and assured. It was good to know what to expect at a time in life when I so often didn't.

When we moved to Florida, I longed for what was familiar and felt estranged from all that was new. Florida, which used to sound so exotic, seemed as remote and unfamiliar as the moon, and I cried every day the first six months I lived there. No amount of motherly cheerfulness, sisterly concern, fatherly apologies for bringing us there, or well-intended advice from friends about getting on with my life was of any use. I shrouded myself in the grief of my loss, and that's where I remained until it took more effort to stay there than to move on.

I think of that time as the four o'clock of my life—the time of changing from one person to another whether I liked it or not. I think of it as the time when, even before we left Indianapolis, I would sit on my bed, looking out the west-facing window and watching the sun sink behind the woods. And I would lie on my bed and cry, just because I needed to, just because the sun was going down. Just because I was fourteen.

Now, ironically, I'm again living in the Florida city to which my parents transplanted me so many years ago, this time by choice. I've taken root here, like the root cutting of a friend's four-o'clock—magenta with cream-colored streaks in it—that's growing nicely in my border right here, right now.

Maybe it's the place where we make that difficult transition from youth to young adult that defines for us where home is. I've spent years in other towns and cities, but this is home. This is where I continue to return, regardless of where my wanderlust leads me. So when I look at the unassuming yet dependable four-o'clock, I see a flower that represents change and homecoming, transplanting and setting down roots, growing and becoming the person I was meant to be all along.

17

Controlling Pests

*The squeamish brush visible pests into a can of kerosene
carried about for the purpose. I crush beetles and aphids
between thumb and forefinger and leave the victims
on the battlefield as a caution. Coming across the
mangled remains of one's kin is evidently as
unpleasant to bugs as it would be to human beings,
and they usually leave the scene.*
—Eleanor Perényi, *Green Thoughts*

Thank goodness the peacocks haven't been coming to my garden lately. As beautiful as they are, they happen to be one of my biggest garden pests.

Our 1956 ranch-style house sits on a road that used to dead-end into an old but productive citrus grove. When the grove went down to the dozers and dump trucks to clear the way for a new multimillion-dollar housing development, we thought the peacocks that had lived in the grove as long as most folks in town could remember would go away too. Despite the peacocks' beauty, the gardener in me let out a secret sigh of relief at the prospect of not having to fight them for my garden anymore.

But like the tangelo tree on the edge of our property that somehow escaped the boundaries of the grove and therefore the fate of its brother and sister trees, the peacocks are still quite comfortable strutting their stuff wherever they please, sleeping in oaks forty feet up, and wandering all over the old neighborhoods as their progenitors did. No iron fence or brick wall can keep them from parading through the streets and yards where generations of peafowl have both bedazzled and bedeviled residents ever since people first settled here.

Some of my neighbors feed the peacocks cat food, seeking to attract them into their yards where they look like living lawn ornaments. It's kind of a "pink flamingo" thing, only in iridescent teals and cobalt blues. Peacocks have a fondness for cat food, I've been told, and all I can figure is that the pansies and petunias they turn into tossed salad as they graze their way through my garden after feeding on Meow Mix at the neighbors' must be a refreshing chaser. There was a time when they took crackers and pretzels from my hand, but when these thirty-pound grazers mistook my hospitality for carte blanche to feast on whatever they might fancy, I withdrew their meal ticket. They assumed my stale breadcrumbs were appetizers on the end of a buffet table I call my garden.

When they started taking out my petunias, I thought, *Okay. Which shall it be? Peacocks or petunias?* The peacocks won, since petunia season was almost over anyway. So I replaced the petunias with salvia and coleus, both of which the peacocks disdained. When they denuded the sunflower stalks as far as their necks could stretch, I planted cosmos in front of the frayed stems, hiding them in frilly foliage that didn't appeal to the birds' finicky palates. But when they took on my two-year-old hydrangea bushes, I cried "fowl" and declared war on the peacocks.

They did not seem to notice.

Every day about midmorning, three males in full plumage would saunter up the road leading from the newly constructed neighborhood to the street in front of my house. As if on cue, all three would turn left and swish into my front yard, dragging their shimmering three-foot tails behind them and heading straight for their favorite snack: hydrangea salad. I tried shooing them out of the garden, but they were often full upon the plants before I spotted them from my kitchen window. I can't live out in the garden from dawn to dusk—much as I would like to—so constant vigilance wasn't the solution. My hydrangeas were peacock-pruned to a raggedy mess before I got more than a couple of pale blue mopheads to bloom for me. What was I to do?

In a fit of desperation and a flash of inspiration, I showed my husband an item called the Bird Banger in a farming catalog. This product, developed to repel Canada geese whenever they flock in and attempt to take out an entire cornfield, involves a kind of gun that shoots a blast of air and noise and delivers a blow guaranteed not to kill or maim the animals but to scare the living daylights out of all "large bird pests." Even though I could never use such a thing, believe me, I was tempted. Just seeing that such a product was available gave me some comfort: I wasn't the only person in the world who didn't love Big Bird.

I finally settled on surrounding my hydrangeas with a fence made of accordion-style tomato cages set far enough out from the plants to keep them beyond neck and beak range. The devastation of my hydrangeas ceased. As luck would have it, mating season beckoned these guys before they had a chance to figure out a way around my flimsy barrier. They migrated back to wherever they stay when Mother Nature calls, proud as, well, you know, and for about five months I was relieved of my peacock-pest problem. By the time mating season was over and they returned, my hydrangeas were well-enough established to withstand their nibbling.

We gardeners are always trying to consider the lesson we might learn when faced with a problem that seems bigger than we are. The Bible is full of stories of crop-destroying plagues—

usually locusts, though; not often peacocks—and entomologists the world over earn their pay concocting ways to rid gardens and fields of insect pests. Plagues of insects are a part of agricultural history, so I don't take the plague of the peacocks personally. What I do consider is whether there is any symbolic meaning behind a problem such as this and whether I'm handling it in the best way.

Gardeners have several choices when dealing with garden pests in general: (1) do nothing, let nature take its course, and hope for minimal damage; (2) attack with pesticides and risk endangering beneficial insects or other critters; (3) lure the pests away by setting out plants they prefer to eat, hoping they'll ignore the ones you really don't want them to destroy; or (4) set up boundaries to keep them from getting to the plants you want to protect. In the case of my peacock pests, since luring them away didn't work and "avianicide" was out of the question, the obvious choice was to set up boundaries they could not or would not want to cross.

Staying Grounded

Setting boundaries is a good way to deal with pests in our lives, whether they're in or out of the garden. Like my peacock visitors, sometimes the people who steal our time and attention, if not our gardens, are attractive as well as invasive. Setting limits on how much we're willing to give to other people's needs is extremely difficult. Creative people in particular tend to be tuned into the world and the people around them. They can be more susceptible to needy friends and family members attempting to appropriate their time and energy. They give themselves away, because meeting the needs of others may seem more important than taking care of their own.

Most people who take part in my "Answering the Creative Call" classes find the lessons on making time and simplifying life among the most useful in the study. But when we talk about the need to set boundaries around their time so they can focus on their art, many get strangely defensive. All that training to think of others before themselves is hard to overcome.

What? Turn off the telephone ringer and let my answering machine take messages while I'm working? Impossible. What if I miss an important call?

Say no to extra commitments? How can I? What if people think I'm not a team player?

Stop trying to solve problems for friends and family who are totally capable of solving them on their own? Won't they think I'm uncaring and self-centered?

We all need silence, solitude, and uninterrupted creative time, but creative people such as gardeners may need even more time than others to make space in their lives to grow spiritually and work on their art, whether that's gardening or something else they feel called to do. And like other artists, gardeners are called to create not just for themselves but for others as well. Consider the poet who writes a piece that touches the hearts of thousands of readers; he had to set boundaries around his time in order to get that poem written. Hasn't he served those who will read his poetry while also serving his talent? In the same way, a painter goes to the studio and puts up her "Do Not Disturb" sign, knowing that unless she sets firm boundaries, she'll be called on to referee every minor family crisis that comes along and never get any painting done. Isn't she serving both her need to create and the people who will someday enjoy her paintings? And won't her family benefit from learning to be more self-sufficient rather than depending on her to do for them what they can do for themselves?

Setting boundaries is about making wise choices. We won't always get it right the first time, because often those "pests" in our lives, like the peacocks I love despite the destruction they wreak on my garden, are people or activities we love. Setting boundaries would not be so hard if it were just about keeping the real pests at bay; it's hard because we don't see those we love as pests. We can also be seduced by our own need to help others, to spill out ourselves for these people we love. It can be more pleasurable—and easier—to spend our energy being the hero for folks than being a servant to the work God has called us to do.

Gardeners, as I've mentioned before, are often accused of being control freaks. We share a need to manage, to order, and to be in charge of what goes on around us. That need to control is the very thing that tempts us to get more involved than we should in the lives of others. Isn't it interesting that while we're willing to do everything we can to manage and even eliminate pests in the garden, we often fail to control the distracters in the rest of our lives?

Soul Gardening

Where do you need to set boundaries in your daily life? Who takes for granted that you'll always sacrifice your needs for theirs, even when it's not really necessary? How can you eliminate some of these distractions in order to be a more creative, more fulfilled person? Pray that you'll find just the right "tomato cages" to set limits and protect your space from the encroachment of others so you can grow into the spiritually mature, creative person God created you to be.

18

Deadheading

Gardening is a kind of deadheading—keeping us from going to seed. The joyful gardener is evidence of an incarnation. One purpose of a garden is to stop time.
—Michael P. Garofalo, *Pulling Onions*

The term "deadheading" may sound like a description of groups of flower children following a certain rock band around the country. It also sounds as though it could mean the practice of sitting around gazing into space while doing nothing at all. Actually, "deadheading" means removing spent flowers after they've bloomed so the plant that produced them will be encouraged to go on blooming.

When I first heard the word and learned what it meant, I smiled at the appropriateness of it. I remembered my mother going through the marigolds she grew along the side of our house in Indianapolis, popping off the faded flower heads before they could set seed. She told me she did that to keep the plants blooming. I realize now that it was about keeping the plants in the moment rather than letting them move on to fruition and decline. Deadheading is about arresting one kind of development in a plant so that it, and we, can enjoy the flowering phase for as long as possible.

So much of gardening has to do with timing. When showers are forecast for late afternoon, I know to transplant or set out plants in the morning so the rain will help set the plants' roots firmly into the soil. I've also learned to weed in the evening, after the rain, when the soil has been moistened and loosened by those afternoon showers. Timing is everything when it comes to transplanting and weeding. Transplant new seedlings on a dry, sunny day, and you can count on fatalities. Wait until the soil dries to the consistency of concrete, and weeding will become a major excavation project.

Deadheading is a bit more forgiving: you usually have a window of opportunity lasting a few days to interrupt the life cycle of your plants and fool them into thinking they need to set more flowers and not just go gently into the good night of seed setting. Although the exact moment of deadheading isn't critical, if you're going to do it at all, you still have to be conscious of the timing.

Here's how it works. When we look at a flowering plant, its flower or blossom strikes us as the crowning jewel, the purpose and goal of the plant. A quick refresher from the botany unit we covered in tenth-grade biology reminds us, however, that the plant's purpose in blooming is to attract pollinators so it can bear fertile seed. Before it flowers and sets seeds, a plant uses the energy stored from photosynthesis for growth. As soon as the flower is fertilized and begins to ripen into seeds, the plant's energy shifts to one thing: assuring the continuity of its species through propagation. The onset of seed production signals the "change of life" for most plants. Once a plant has generated seeds, it knows it has served its function and will begin to decline and die. Deadheading is a way to prolong both the plant and its flower production by postponing the seed-producing phase.

Like most gardening tasks, deadheading takes a bit of practice. The best way to learn is to follow an experienced gardener making his or her deadheading rounds. Most gardeners carry a pair of pruning sheers or nippers and a bucket with them whenever they walk through the garden. Each decapitated flower head goes into the bucket, since garden waste left on the ground around plants tends to encourage unwanted insect and fungal development. The "deadheads" then go into the compost heap, except for thorny stems, which take too long to break down and whose barbs can come back, even years later, to haunt you.

Most *determinate* plants such as daylilies, irises, and spring-flowering bulbs do not continue to set flowers after they have finished blooming for the season, but cutting back the spent stems will allow the plant's energy to go to root and leaf production rather than to seeding. This encourages the plants to mature, spread, and produce even more blooms the following season. When you remove the flower heads after they've bloomed, the plant will put energy that would have gone to seeding into multiplying its bulbs underground, and that's what we want. It takes at least two years for a daffodil *seed* to grow into a bulb capable of blooming, but a *bulb* generated underground from a parent plant will usually bloom the following year, often making more bulbs underground in the process. In more southerly zones, there is another benefit of deadheading spent flower stalks: many plants in the iris and daylily families will send up new flower scrapes and will bloom more than once in a season if they aren't allowed to make seeds. Their programming tells them to keep trying to propagate, and cutting off the seed pods before they mature triggers another attempt to produce flowers.

Most annuals are *indeterminate,* which means they continue to grow and produce more flower heads even while they're flowering. These should be cut back just above a healthy-looking leaf at the strongest part of the stem or just above a node where a new stem is already forming. A new stem will develop just below the cut, and a new bud will form at the end of it. You can dead-head some plants, like marigolds and petunias, by simply popping off the entire flower, including the receptacle, which is the base of the flower where its seeds are produced. Remember that the purpose of deadheading is to remove all the baby-making machinery from the plant after each flower is spent so the plant will stop developing seeds and start producing more flowers. Deadhead most plants by making cuts that take off not only the flower heads but part of the stem as well.

Deadheading tea roses takes a bit of practice, but there's a simple trick to it. As soon as a rose begins fading, cut it back to just above the first leaf consisting of five leaflets. If possible, choose one that points to the outside of the plant, as the new stem tends to grow in the direction of the leaf above which you make your cut. By making your cut above a five-leaflet leaf pointing to the outside of the bush, you'll be able to keep your rose bushes open and airy. You'll also manage to keep stems from crisscrossing and abrading one another.

Florabunda and grandiflora roses have several blooms clustered on the end of the same stem. They don't all bloom at once, so with these clustering roses I simply remove the individual blossoms as they start declining. When the last blossom fades, I cut back the whole stem to the most likely looking five-leaflet leaf, just as with tea roses. Experience and common sense will give you the confidence you need to become a ruthless dead-header in no time.

I love the practice of deadheading, because it gets me out into the garden on days when I really don't have time to spend hours in the garden. No need to get into my work clothes, put up my hair, put on sunscreen and insect repellant, or get out my tool bucket. Some days I need to get outdoors, to feel the air, to smell the earth, even though I may have only ten or fifteen minutes to spare. That's when I like to do my deadheading. What a great way to start the day before shifting gears and getting into my commute to work. What a pleasant way to spend a few minutes while supper is on the stove or to end an evening just as the sun goes down.

Whenever I'm cutting back spent blossoms, I enjoy the feeling that in taking something away from a plant, I'm actually giving it something: I'm prolonging its existence and keeping it healthy and beautiful. I'm helping it remain in the present and keeping it from rushing headlong into the next phase of its life.

Staying Grounded

Deadheading plants reminds me that in order to keep my own life healthy, balanced, and growth-producing, I need to remain centered in the now rather than rushing into the next thing. Each time we cut a declining or already-going-to-seed blossom off a plant, we're encouraging new growth in other areas of the plant; we're promoting its overall health.

Similarly, sometimes in our own lives we need to stop, to remain in the moment, to be still and cease striving in order to strengthen our overall health.

"To everything there is a season, A time for every purpose under heaven" (Ecclesiastes 3:1, NKJV). The time is not always ripe for seeing something through to fruition. It's hard for us to realize this in our goal-directed world. Is it possible that there are times we need just to blossom and flower where we are? Can it be that we sometimes need to keep blooming again and again until we're finished with a phase of our life and it's time to move on? In our rush to completion and achievement, perhaps we miss a kind of strengthening and maturing that can be realized only through the interruption of our natural inclination toward new accomplishments.

Soul Gardening

How does it feel to "be still and know" that God is God and you are not? This is a hard one for gardeners, because we're goal-oriented by nature. We check our gardens several times a day just to see what has happened in the last few hours. Patience is something gardening teaches us.

Think of one area of your life in which you might profit from staying in the moment rather than striving toward the next goal. Write or talk about that area, or simply consider that new realization the next time you deadhead your garden.

19

Evening Primrose
Oenothera speciosa

*Beyond its practical aspects, gardening—
be it of the soil or soul—can lead us on a philosophical
and spiritual exploration that is nothing less
than a journey into the depths of our own sacredness
and the sacredness of all beings.*
—Christopher McDowell, *The Sanctuary Garden*

The pink evening primrose, *Oenothera speciosa,* in contrast to its yellow cousin, *Oenothera biennis,* is a compact shrub whose flowers open up in the early evening and release a wonderful fragrance once the sun goes down. Its flowers start out almost white, then turn rosy pink with darker pink veins as they age. From the buttery-colored center of each blossom rises a four-branched stamen that is common to all species of *Oenothera.* Most night-blooming plants are pale, almost ghostly in color, and that's no accident. Moths and other nocturnal insects must pollinate night bloomers like *Oenothera,* so a whitish color that "glows in the dark" and a strong fragrance are necessary to attract these beneficial insects.

I grow evening primrose on the border of my garden because I so love the ethereal look and smell of the plant. That it attracts night-ranging pollinators is another bonus. Picture a plant that gets anywhere from one to two feet tall, can spread up to fifteen inches across, and will send runners beyond that to form other plants vegetatively (from its roots). The blossoms remain open and fragrant until morning, and they may remain open all day when the sky is overcast. Growing this plant increases the number of hours in the day when my garden is interesting. Gardeners who don't grow night-blooming plants don't know what they're missing.

Pink evening primrose is native to the south-central United States, especially the rocky prairies and savannas of the lower Midwest, but like the daylily, evening primroses have been naturalized throughout the world. They grow well in almost any kind of soil, which is great except for the fact that they can be surreptitiously invasive. "Evening primroses generally prefer dry, sandy soil. They get by in such habitats because their roots are capable of storing water. Eager to self-sow, once these biennials get in the yard, they will be around for years to come."[1] If you're not careful, you can end up with too much of a good thing.

Evening primrose is easily propagated via root division. You can also allow them to proliferate on their own as their roots spread underground and emerge as new plants a short distance from the parent plant. Pink evening primroses are also easy to grow from seed, but that's not necessary if you have one good stock plant.

Growing as they do in low mounds, evening primroses are perfect edging plants for woodland trails, rock gardens, wildflower meadows, and naturalistic borders, although they do prefer full sun. Their flowers don't open until after dark, but the plants themselves need sunlight for their roots, stems, and leaves to flourish. In early morning, when their flowers are still open, they attract bees, moths, and hummingbirds, but because they're night bloomers, nocturnal insects such as moths are their primary pollinators.

What's my fascination with this plant? As I've said, evening is not my best time of the day. In bed by nine-thirty and up by five, I would miss the night bloomers altogether if most of them didn't open up early in the evening and stay open until the morning. What I like is growing plants that perfume the air whatever the time of day. I live in a neighborhood of walkers and runners, many of whom are nocturnal. Whenever I have trouble sleeping, I'll look out the window, and within a few minutes will see someone walk or run by; I've seen them at all hours between sundown and sunup. I wonder if they're night-shift workers just home, insomniacs, or simply folks who would rather exercise in the cool of the darkness than the heat of the day.

I like to think that I'm giving these night owls an unexpected gift when they pass by my gardens and take in the fragrance of the evening primrose, blooming ghostly pink under the streetlight. I like to think that along with the song of the tree frogs and the cicada, along with apparitions of other pale-colored night bloomers in my garden, a whiff of something heavenly might make a difference for these late-night folks.

Not only do plants such as evening primrose, night-blooming cereus, and moonflower attract nocturnal pollinators, but they also attract other insects, like mosquitoes, which in turn attract bats. Bats eat their weight in insects every night, and they especially love mosquitoes. Although I doubt my late-night exercising neighbors are even aware of these wonderful creatures circling their heads as they speed by my gardens, the plants give them the gift of fewer mosquitoes to harass them on their run. I'm aware of this, even if my neighbors are not.

I also like the idea that even while I'm asleep, my garden is working for balance and health in my little part of the world.

People who garden only in backyards behind fences and walls miss the pleasure of watching neighbors slow down to admire their handiwork. When I'm working outside and someone says, "I just want you to know how much I enjoy walking by your gardens every day," I often reply, "Thank you for saying so. One reason I garden is so people like you can enjoy the beauty too."

Sometimes a neighbor will introduce himself or herself and ask about a specific plant or pose a garden question. I offer to share my extras with other gardeners, and that's another real joy for me. I've even found anonymous gifts left in my garden: a start of plumeria one time and a metal sculpture of a garden fairy with a note that read, "Thanks to the garden angel for making this beautiful spot." I've received letters in my mailbox asking me how I get my hydrangeas to bloom so profusely. My most recent mystery gift was a small concrete armadillo!

Like most gardeners, I garden because I can't help myself. I garden because I want to offer a little beauty, a little "organized chaos" in this often chaotic and ugly world. So, be it for the runners, the babies in carriages, the moths, or the bats, the scent of an evening primrose in bloom is an offering and a contribution to making the world just a little more lovely. Morning, afternoon, or evening, it's what we gardeners do.

20

Pruning

*If a person cannot love a plant after he has
pruned it, then he has either done a
poor job or is devoid of emotion.*
—Liberty Hyde Bailey, *Manual of Gardening*

The rains came back this summer, and my flowers, shrubs, and
trees are growing out of control. Wild branches stick up in every
direction. Bushes and perennial flowers have doubled in size in
the past two weeks of wet abundance. Trees are growing suckers, or "water sprouts." When growth becomes this excessive,
it's time to get out the pruning sheers and rein in the garden: to
cut back, sometimes ruthlessly, and get those plants into shape.

Pruning is similar to deadheading, but the goals of pruning
have more to do with the health and structure of each plant than
simply removing flowers past their prime to prolong flowering.
When we prune a shrub or tree, our purposes are threefold:

1. Architectural: to remove any branches or limbs that cross
   or rub against others or go off in directions that make
   the plant look unbalanced. Pruning controls the height
   and spread of plants and allows you to create a shape that
   pleases you.

2. Therapeutic: to take out dead or diseased branches or limbs as well as any suckers that may, well, suck energy from the plant while contributing nothing positive to it.

3. Horticultural: to improve the quality, size, and yield of flowers and fruit. You'll normally get larger and more plentiful blossoms on a compact plant than you will on one that spreads all over the place.

Mark Nelson of Nelson Roses says, "Pruning is the removal of damaged, weak, or otherwise unnecessary growth to promote good health and a pleasant appearance. This is based on an understanding of how the [plant] grows . . . and the wisdom of an experienced gardener, as opposed to the rest of us who are best classified as butchers."[1] I've found his admission to be sadly true. The advent of electric hedge trimmers has turned the same people who might have been plant sculptors into plant manglers. Pruning is an art that combines knowledge of your plant with a good eye for harmony, symmetry, and beauty. This means taking time to look at the overall shape of the plant, then judiciously removing the parts that detract from that ideal. Power tools rarely accomplish this kind of artistic shaping.

I was recently driving through Polk County in the center of Florida, where thousands of citrus groves still thrive. The natural shape of most citrus trees is roughly round, and until recently groves keepers pruned their trees according to what looked natural. Not so today. I felt as though I'd driven "through the looking glass" as I passed row after row of box-shaped trees. I realized immediately the reason for the cubical shape in commercial groves: it's easier for the giant mechanical pruners to move down a row and make straight cuts from one tree to the next, like mowing a lawn sideways, than to prune trees individually and keep them spherical. I could also see that the fruit would be easier to harvest from trees that were flat on their tops and sides. For the sake of the people who labor in these groves, I forgave this assault on the eye. But hexahedral citrus trees? Too weird for me.

This tendency toward expediency over artistry evidences itself in commercially managed home landscapes, too. Just when the plumbago hedge near my house becomes dense with the sky-blue blossoms that characterize it, along come the commercial landscapers, sheering the whole thing back to a rounded-off haystack. It will take two weeks for those plants to regain their composure. Just behind the plumbagos are a stand of my favorite bush roses, "Knockout," famous for their carefree habit and omnipresent blooms. They get regularly mutilated as well, and I've yet to see the advantage of this arbitrary shaping, other than the convenience of the landscapers.

I deadhead mine, then prune the entire bush in the spring and fall, and my bushes are twice as large as those commercially pruned ones. And while those in commercial landscapes are continually recovering from their aggressive prunings, mine are almost always covered with blossoms. The sculpted borders and hedges of many homes in my town suggest human contrivance rather than the rambling disposition of the natural world.

Careful and judicious pruning by hand is the gardener's attempt to impose order on chaos while respecting the form and function of each individual plant in the landscape. For instance, part of garden lore here in Florida is that pruning should be done on Valentine's Day; although we don't get many frosts, if we're going to get one, it's not likely to occur after February 14. So I prune my shrubs and rose bushes on Valentine's Day. I enjoy the rhythm of the seasons and the idea that certain things occur at specific times of the year, and adhering to a date for a particular garden chore keeps me in tune with the cadence of natural time. Pruning—especially my roses—on Valentine's Day seems appropriate, and it's been done that way here for generations.

After the danger of our infrequent frosts has passed, I take a look at the crape myrtles and citrus trees and give them a good shaping. I start by removing any dead wood and sucker shoots as close to the trunk as I can. Scratching the top layer of bark with my thumbnail will usually reveal any live green tissue and keep me from taking out an otherwise well-placed branch that simply looks dead. If no signs of life appear, the branch is history. After removing dead branches, I get rid of any branches that are causing structural problems: those growing toward the center of the plant rather than outward, or those that cross and rub against other branches. Finally, I cut the whole plant down to size by taking each branch back to form a pleasing shape and to keep the plant from growing beyond my ability to care for it.

Studying the plants you're working with will help you learn how far back to take each plant you're pruning. Keep in mind that a pleasing shape does not have to be round, conical, or rectangular. I sometimes prune my azaleas to look like large bonsai, with clouds of leaves puffing out around the main stem. Observe the way trees and bushes look in their natural setting and try replicating these shapes in your garden.

A radical method of pruning known as "renewal pruning" should be used only on plants that you're likely to lose anyway. This technique involves giving the plant a severe cutting to within inches of the ground so that it can start over and grow bushy again. It can take as long as three years for some plants to recover fully from this ruthless pruning, but the plant will look brand new if the operation is successful.

Even experienced gardeners can dread the process of pruning, because it seems so pitiless. But once you get the hang of it and see how much better your plants look a couple of weeks later, it starts to feel good. You realize that what you're doing is contributing to a healthier, more balanced, more beautiful garden.

Staying Grounded

We all have areas of our lives where we need to prune away the things that are holding us back and keeping us from being as beautiful, as healthy, and as well-managed as we're capable of being. I know I have some "branches" in my life that are at cross-purposes with my overall vision and plan, branches that rub against and deter the growth of what would be wholesome and balanced if I could just bring myself to cut them out.

If pressed, most of us will admit that we're overcommitted and don't make time to do what's important for us to flourish. In my book *The Creative Call,* I talk about simplifying our lives in order to find time to practice our art. One suggestion I make is that we learn not to be slaves to the telephone and e-mail. Another idea is to make a list of what's most important to us and see what we can prune from our busy schedules to make time to do these things. Is it more important to work in the garden or to keep a perfect house? Do the kids really need to be involved in so many activities, or is it more important for them to have downtime and for us to have time to write, paint, or practice a musical instrument? Just as we prune our trees and bushes, we must decide what to cut out of our lives so that we have time for the things that matter.

Unfortunately, just as pruning the hibiscus that's in full bloom but is blocking the walkway to the front door is hard, it's difficult to cut out activities and back away from commitments that deprive us of the time we need for what really matters. You can't exactly tell the acquaintance who wants a couple of hours of your attention each week to talk about the same problems she's been having for years that you can't be her therapist anymore. But you can say, "I'm not booking any lunches or dates right now until I get caught up with some important things that I have to make time for." Learning to gently say no to things like this is a way of reducing the outflow of our energy so that we can concentrate on making the core parts of our lives healthier and richer.

Soul Gardening

Say this prayer when you need help cutting back on the things that are getting in the way of your growth and development: *Lord, help me see where I need to cut back so what's important might flourish. Give me wisdom, discernment, and the courage to say no to the things that are less worthy of my time and energy. Grant me the assurance that when I prune away some of the things I take on out of guilt and obligation, you'll honor my desire to spend that time on the things that really matter. May it be so.*

21

Rooting

*The only limit to your garden is
at the boundaries of your imagination.*
—Thomas D. Church, Grace Hall, Michael Laurie
Gardens Are for People

If you've been gardening for any length of time, you probably already realize that gardening can be an expensive habit to maintain. I once entered several months of household receipts into a money-management computer program, and I was astounded to realize that in six months I had spent as much on gardening as groceries! (Needless to say, I must figure out how to cut back on the groceries.) At the beginning of the growing season, gardeners lay out money for soil amendments, seed, mulch, and basic equipment, but the biggest recurring expense is buying plants. After all, the fastest way to translate the garden you see in your mind into a garden you see out your window is to buy plants and set them out in your well-prepared beds. *Voilà!* Instant garden!

But if you're like me and live on a limited budget, you have to find alternatives to purchasing costly plants each time you see a specimen you just have to have. Seeding is the least expensive way to go, but planting seeds doesn't lead to an instant garden. Gardeners, like other artists, get a vision and want to see it in a tangible form right away. By the time you've noticed what's in bloom in someone else's yard, it's often too late to start those plants from seed. So how do you avoid going into bankruptcy in order to satisfy your craving for new plants? The answer is rooting.

Rooting is a type of asexual propagation that involves taking cuttings from a parent plant—pieces of their roots, bulbs, leaves, or stems—and rooting them in order to create a clone of the parent. "[That these] small fragments of stems, leaves, or roots that form new roots of their own . . . these chips off the old block somehow grow to become the block itself is equally as thrilling as a seed's journey into planthood."[1] Rooting stem cuttings to create new plants from old is one of the most creative and enjoyable activities a gardener can engage in outside the garden. It's also a great way to get your hands dirty without getting sunstroke in the simmering heat of summer.

Any plant, shrub, herb, or tree that forms root nodules along its stems wherever they touch the ground will make a great candidate for rooting. Look around everywhere you go, and take cuttings of likely contenders. Once you get the rooting bug, every new plant you encounter will appear to you as a parent or stock plant.

I love rooting plants from cuttings. It's easy and essentially free. I've successfully rooted just about every kind of softwood plant I've attempted, from bougainvilleas to crape myrtles, from roses to honeysuckle, from geraniums to impatiens. In the humidity of summer, folks take cuttings from my coleus plants, dip their stems in rooting compound—a hormone powder that stimulates root growth—and stick the cutting directly into the garden, where it forms roots and grows into a new plant. I've also been able to beg or pinch cuttings from parent bushes in neighbors' borders, from commercial landscapes, and even along roadsides.

Right now it's mid-July in Florida, and I'm anticipating a couple more months of high summer. Many of my flowering plants will decline in the next few weeks, but I have a plan to replace declining dahlias with brightly colored coleus. I'm rooting coleus cuttings from all over town. If I see a variety I find interesting—not all of them are, in my opinion—I ask the owner if I might have two or three cuttings from the plant, and I offer to trade her for some of mine. Without exception, homeowners are delighted that I like their choice in landscaping materials enough to want to take a bit of it home with me for my own garden.

I have to confess to snipping a cutting or two from plants and bushes that line roadways and parking lots. These plants, I tell myself, need to be pinched back anyway so they won't get leggy and unattractive. This pinching back wherever I go has been a compulsion of mine for years. I've been known to deadhead a whole planter of marigolds outside a shopping mall while waiting to meet someone, not for any reason other than I can't stand to see plants going into decline because no one is taking the time to pinch back the spent blossoms. If I snip back a plant that also makes a good candidate for rooting, well then, what's the harm? Walking through my neighborhood, I wonder if I'll find a coleus I've never seen before; part of the joy of gardening is stalking whatever is free for the asking. Another part of the joy lies in the friendships you strike up with other gardeners as you look at the results of one another's work and share the bounty and the beauty of one another's efforts.

If you paint, write, sculpt, or play a musical instrument, what you create is unique and, one hopes, beautiful. The same is true of gardening. Whenever I'm offered a cutting I can root, I feel as though I'm being given free art. I compliment you on your pussy willow tree with its soft, velvety catkins just blooming in the spring, and you say, "Here. Let me get you some cuttings. Root them in water, and then you can have a tree of your own." You admire my stand of hydrangeas, and I offer you some cuttings for your table that you can later root so you'll have hydrangeas of your own next year. What a neighborly system!

Staying Grounded

The garden is a living, breathing thing, and the more of it you give away, the healthier it grows. Just as deadheading and pruning encourage new growth, offering and accepting cuttings for rooting benefits not only the recipient of the material but also the parent plant from which the cutting was taken. When I cut someone a volunteer cleome or dig up a blue plumbago sprout that's crowding my roses, I'm passing on the riches and helping my own garden as well. The more you share your art with others, the prettier you make the world, including your own little part of it.

When we hoard what we have, so often what we're left with rots or becomes a burden to us. When we give things away, our own load is lightened, and we brighten someone else's life at the same time. Albert Einstein said, "It is every man's obligation to put back into the world at least the equivalent of what he takes out of it."[2] We do this as a matter of course when we're gardeners. We give our gardens toil, time, and attention to the details of good gardening, and in return our gardens give us flowers, food, beauty, oxygen, and a place on which the eye can rest and through which the spirit is rejuvenated. Whether we share what we grow, what we have, or what we are, we're fulfilling a purpose for which we were placed on this earth: to give of ourselves. When we share what we have, we often find that we give a gift to ourselves as much as we give one to someone else.

Soul Gardening

Walk through your garden and look at all the plants from which you might take cuttings. Try rooting a few of them and giving them away as gifts. Make generosity a part of your gardening practice, and let that practice flow over into the rest of your life.

22

Night-Blooming Cereus

Hylocereus undatus

I do know that there are people who are like flowers,
just as simply in touch with God and as incarnate with
His spirit as the flowers; and I do know that there is no
greater thrill that one can get than by reaching out
and touching these great souls.
—George Washington Carver
The Man Who Talked with the Flowers

The last time I visited northwest Arkansas, where I lived from 1973 to 1986, I left with several cuttings of plants tucked in plastic bags in my carry-on luggage. One of the plants was given to me by George and Mona, friends of my youth: a night-blooming cereus, which is now thriving in my Florida garden.

Mona and I are in our fifties now, but to me she's still the twenty-something friend with whom I shared the joys and trials of new motherhood. Like me, she wanted to wait to have children until it seemed financially feasible. Like me, she went ahead and had them even though it never was. We were of that tribe of back-to-nature folk who took a vow of poverty in the seventies and went to the country to live off the land. Prosperity was neither a motivation nor a result of our efforts. Building our houses with money earned rather than borrowed, we were always just one step ahead of winter: hanging insulation even when there was no money for Sheetrock to cover it; setting up the wood-burning stove and cleaning out the flue or chimney right before the icy winds started blowing; finally shingling the roof after years of hearing black paper slap against the decking in the wind; cutting enough firewood to last through the season; and insulating water pipes to keep them from freezing. Everything we did cost time, energy, and money, so we never would have had children had we not taken a leap of faith.

When I was thirty and Mona was twenty-seven, we discovered we would be having babies within a month of each other. Even though Mona and George already had one child, Jason, our both being pregnant at the same time naturally brought us closer. But what we had in common went beyond expecting new babies. We had come to the mountains for the same reasons: to live unpretentiously and to get away from too many people and too much competition for too little space and too few resources. We came to breathe pure air and drink clean water, to live among woods and wildflowers, to learn to live in friendship with nature. And we both had made the sacrifices demanded by this rich but difficult life for the sake, at least in part, of the children we had yet to conceive.

After Mona's son Travis was born in February and my son, James, arrived in March, a deep friendship emerged. Mona and her family lived on forty acres on the side of a mountain. A creek ran through their rocky land, and nearby they had built a cabin with their own hands. James's father and I lived on twenty-five mountaintop acres in a hand-built house of our own. Travis and

James were both born into a world of gardens and would lie on blankets in the shade, looking up into clumps of frosty purple blueberries or the grass green of young cornstalks while we mothers worked beside them, tending our gardens and keeping food on the table.

Some afternoons Mona and I tore ourselves away from the endless chores required just to get by and met at a favorite swimming hole to give our boys—and ourselves—a break from the sweltering northwest Arkansas summer. Other days we would drag children, jars, and produce to the local cannery and help each other put up the harvest while the boys ran around outside. Most holidays brought all the back-to-the-land families together for potlucks, bonfires, sing-alongs, and horseshoes, with kids often outnumbering the adults. Mona and I lived too far apart to call ourselves neighbors, but the common threads of our lives kept knitting us together.

When our boys were about five, Mona decided to get her horticulture degree at a nearby university. Going back to college in her thirties was a huge decision for her, but I helped by editing her writing as she read her English essays to me over the phone during our regular Saturday morning calls. One day years later, after I had moved back to Florida and our phone calls were less frequent, she phoned me to say, "I *did* it! I graduated with my degree in horticulture!" Mona's perseverance to finish something she had dreamed of was typical of the friend I knew.

Returning to visit a place where you lived for thirteen years can be a bittersweet thing. I had left Arkansas during the death throes of a terminally ill marriage, seeking safety and solace in family and friends on the East Coast. The exuberance of the young visionaries who had settled those hills and hollows had mellowed into hunkering down to whatever life we had made for ourselves. I was leaving the isolation of the mountain to save my marriage or, short of that, to be in a safe place when it failed. As time passed, most of the other back-to-the-landers either moved to town or returned to the places from which they had originally come. Those hand-built houses became weekend retreats from the city life we almost all ended up settling for.

When James and Travis were both twelve, I made a trip back to Arkansas to visit my old friends. I thought I was ready, but this trip to the mountains only six years after such a painful leaving was still difficult for me. Not enough time had passed. Too much reminded me of why I had left—and not enough helped me remember why I had gone there to begin with.

Ten more years came and went before I returned again. I called Mona when I got to Little Rock and proposed a short visit to see her in northwest Arkansas. We had a lot of catching up to do. During the past sixteen years, we had slid into one of those once-a-year-Christmas-card friendships, and I hadn't heard from her for the last couple of holidays. The last time she had written, she had told me that Travis, who was then eighteen, was in recovery from a rare form of bone cancer. I naively assumed that's where things still were, that Travis was a cancer survivor.

"How *are* you, dear Mona?" I asked excitedly when she answered her phone.

She guardedly replied, "Okay, under the circumstances."

"What circumstances?" I asked, my heart starting to pound in dread.

"Well, you know, everything with Travis and all. It's been pretty rough."

"I knew he had been sick. But he's okay now, isn't he?"

"Janice . . . Travis *died*."

I went through the rest of the weekend a heartbeat away from tears. In the morning and afternoon we spent together driving through the dazzling Ozark Mountains in autumn, visiting all the places that were once home for us, we talked about Travis and wept together as though he had just died. It occurred to me that this was one reason I had made this trip: it was good for Mona and George to be with someone so freshly, heart-torn-openly grieved over Travis's death. We sat together and cried through a video made by a cancer research organization during the time Travis was alive, in treatment, and in remission. George told me he hadn't been able to watch the video since before Travis's death. In our shared brokenness, a new thing was born in my heart: an acute awareness of the preciousness and fragility of these loved ones who are given into our care for such a little, little while.

Another insight was born in me that day: while Mona and I were growing up as young adults together, we were, without knowing it, growing into old, old friends. And old friends are the ones who can truly share the deep things, because old friends were with you during that time you were growing into who you would become. I knew then that I had come back to the mountains for my own healing, to realize I had grown beyond the pain of the last few years I had lived there. I was able to recognize and remember what had drawn me there in the first place. But I had also come back so that Mona could be with an old friend who could stand by her side in her sorrow.

The first year I lived in the mountains, I learned a song from a girl with a dog and a fiddle who stopped for a visit at a cabin in the woods where we were living. She only stayed the night, but she shared with me a couple of lines of the lyrics in a Hoyt Axton song, the essence of which are that it's the strength we share as we're growing that gives us what we need most.

It was the gift of years that allowed Mona and me to share strength with each other that autumn. When I said good-bye to her at the end of our visit, Mona gave me the start of a night-blooming cereus. I got it home intact and planted it in front of a south-facing wall in my Florida garden. It's a tough, leathery-leafed plant, a member of the cactus family, and it can climb a fence or content itself with bushing out in a pot, multiplying and creating community. After dark, from time to time, it produces a huge waxy blossom, a white flower as ghostly as moon glow that scents the air and startles the eye of anyone out walking late. It blooms one night, and then it's gone.

Whenever I look at or touch or smell this plant, I think of my late-blooming friend Mona with her tender, tough heart gentled by loss. I think of this flower that blooms spectacularly for just one night, reminding me of the preciousness of our children and those who pass through our lives with such beauty and swiftness. I think of George, who has been Mona's backbone through all the triumphs and tragedies of their time together. I think of this plant as an emblem of all those dear old friends who thrive and endure, who not only survive but continue to blossom and flourish, who brighten the days and nights of all who know them, whatever life deals them, who give each other the strength that we share while we're growing—these "night-blooming cereuses" in my life.

23

Watering

[O God], you care for the land and water it;
you enrich it abundantly. . . .
You drench its furrows and level its ridges;
you soften it with showers and bless its crops.
—Psalm 65:9–10

It rained this evening. The skies brooded all afternoon, gathering up thunderheads that taunted and teased everyone suffering in this drought-parched place. Before sunset, just after the sun beamed eerily between a low steel gray cloud bank and the horizon, thunder growled, first far away, then closer. Lightning tore open the sky and the thirsty earth was blessed with a long-awaited drenching. This evening I didn't water my garden.

When my family moved to Florida in 1965, this is the way it was. As inevitable as summertime humidity, an afternoon deluge would come out of nowhere, the wind whipping the sudden downpour from one direction to another, pounding first against the north side of the house, then thrumming on the west windows. It would shift to the east before sheeting the south windows, then hammer the roof straight on, drumming the living room skylight with the relentlessness of a machine-gun attack. As suddenly as it had arrived, the storm would move on, dragging in blue skies and sunshine behind it.

I grew to expect these near-daily downpours that flooded streets and overran swimming pools. This is the way Florida weather used to work. This mini-monsoon season is the reason that until recently more of Florida was under water than high and dry. It's the reason Florida was once known for its clear streams, clean lakes, vast wetlands, and fresh drinking water. The system, when it's working, goes something like this: Rainwater percolates down through layers of sand and limestone, like a kid's science project, seeping into the Florida aquifer, a huge, natural holding tank miles underground. From the aquifer it burbles back to the surface via myriad springs into rivers, lakes, and wells. This is how it functioned before the dredging and draining of wetlands, the paving over of open spaces, and the overpopulating began.

Then, as if to underscore the problem, came the drought.

For four years we were in a state of unprecedented dry weather, and for gardeners that meant learning how to make every drop of water count. I sometimes think about the novel *Dune* as I stand outside hand-watering my gardens with hose and water wand, getting every droplet right to the base of each plant, unwilling to waste even a thimbleful of the precious liquid by using sprinklers. Spraying hither and yon with irrigation systems may appear to emulate nature's capricious rainstorms, but in a dry year the evaporation factor makes sprinkling a waste. Mulching and direct hand watering are acts of conservation, compassion, consciousness, and responsibility.

Plants, like people, can survive weeks without food. But just like people, plants soon wither and fail without adequate water. Water runs right through our sandy Florida soil, so rainfall is a blessing we gardeners never take for granted. I water with a hose whenever I have the time, using well water rather than costly chlorinated city water. I try to practice good stewardship of this precious natural resource by choosing plants that are tolerant of dry conditions. I mulch deeply, water deeply but not widely, and enrich my soil to increase its capacity for holding moisture.

Even though we may not have had rain in weeks, I often hear weather reporters cheerfully proclaim, "Looks like we have another gorgeous day here in sunny central Florida. No rain in sight." I want to scream at that person, "What's the matter with you? Another day without rain is not a 'gorgeous' day! Don't you ever go outside? Don't you see the wetlands drying up, the streams and lakes shrinking, the parched lawns browning, and the danger of wildfire lurking? Get out of your air-conditioned office and take a look at the *real* world!" Okay, I admit I get a tiny bit testy at times.

But we live in a time where convenience tends to trump conscience, and many of us have grown lazy about responsibilities that go along with how we use water. According to Catriona Tudor Erler in *The Frugal Gardener*, watering conservatively is absolutely essential "in these days of shrinking aquifers and population pressure. About half the water consumed by the average homeowner is used to water the yard and garden. . . . Efficient watering means money saved as well as healthier plants."[1] When we water deeply twice a week, we not only reduce evaporation—we encourage deep root formation, and that makes for hardier plants.

In the Hebrew Bible, someone who is blessed by God, who is well rooted in the truth, is often compared to a tree planted by water. Psalm 1:1–3 reads, "Oh, the joys of those who . . . delight in doing everything the LORD wants. . . . They are like trees planted along the riverbank, bearing fruit each season without fail. Their leaves never wither, and in all they do, they prosper" (NLT). Trees planted by water have the advantage of their roots growing into soil that's wet to a great depth. Roots will plow down as deep as the moisture goes. That's why watering deeply and mulching thickly are such good gardening practices. The deeper the root system, the stronger the plant.

Staying Grounded

Our gardens cannot live without water, but too much water drowns the plants' roots and causes plants to rot. Too much water cuts off needed oxygen to root systems, and the whole structure of a plant can suffer, even unto death. As in so many things, it's all about balance.

When I dig holes for new plants, I sometimes see that after the first two or three inches of moist soil, there's nothing but sandy, dry earth, so I know what awaits the root system of a plant that's shallowly watered. On the other hand, I've killed plants with the kindness, waterlogging their root systems until they drowned.

Watering might be compared to feeding our spirits. When faith runs deep, our roots grow healthy. We're grounded, we have a sound foundation, and we enjoy a sense of stability that we don't have when our faith is shallow. Whatever our method of incorporating faith into our lives, the important thing is for us not to just sprinkle on a little prayer or meditation, going through the motions but not getting "down there" where soul changes can happen. It takes time, attention, and *intention* for us to grow spiritually. It's better to spend quality time just a few days a week seeking relationship with God than to mouth superficial platitudes every single day that may assuage the conscience but do nothing to deepen our faith.

Part of this deep watering involves prayer and meditation; part of it is putting our actions where our beliefs are. Isaiah 58:10–11 says,

> If you spend yourselves in behalf of the hungry and satisfy the needs of the oppressed, then your light will rise in the darkness, and your night will become like the noonday. The LORD will guide you always; he will satisfy your needs

in a sun-scorched land and will strengthen your frame. You will be like a well-watered garden, like a spring whose waters never fail.

When we water our gardens, we're extending grace to our plants, our soil, and all the living things in that soil. When we water our souls with prayer, meditation, and doing good works, we open ourselves to grace, and we extend grace to others.

Soul Gardening

The most important time to water our gardens is when new seedlings and transplants are struggling to establish themselves. Until their roots have gone deep and settled into their new environment, the least bit of water deprivation will stress them, perhaps even fatally. Think about a time when you were getting established in a new home, school, job, or relationship. What kind of "watering" did you need until you felt you could make it on your own? When times like these come along, give yourself extra-deep watering by being gracious to yourself rather than self-critical. List all the metaphors for water you can think of, and take time to thank God for all the sources of watering in your life.

24

Weeding

*I always think of my sins when I weed. They grow apace
in the same way and are harder still to get rid of.*
—Helena Rutherfurd Ely, *A Woman's Hardy Garden*

I move methodically through each section of the garden, sometimes kneeling, sometimes sitting on an overturned milk crate,
as I poke the soil with my Japanese weeding knife. The blade tip
catches and dislodges the roots of each oxalis plant, a shamrock-
like plant that has become an invasive exotic in my part of the
country. I toss each excised plant into my bucket, careful not
to lose even one of its clever little bulbs, knowing that given a
chance, it would worm its way back into the heart of my garden and begin again the insidious process of weed propagation,
wild-thing regeneration. The goal, though never fully realized,
is to purge the garden of unwanted plants so that the desirable
ones will have less competition for space, water, and nutrients.
But weeds will return, and there's the rub.

The complaint I hear most on people's "Why I Don't Garden" list is their aversion to the seemingly never-ending chore of weeding. I take a different tack on this subject, finding pleasure in this humble—some would say mind-numbing—task. Neighbors shake their heads and offer condolences that I'm out weeding "again," but I surprise them by saying I enjoy it. Weeding gets me down on my knees and close to the earth, a posture and proximity that—in my out-of-garden life—I rarely assume. The process of weeding is a kind of reverential cleansing for both the garden and me.

When I was a little girl, I preferred playing on dirt piles to anything I could do indoors. I loved the smell of the huge mountain of composted manure at Wallitch Nursery and spent hours with other kids playing "King of the Manure Pile." To this day, the fragrance of rich, loamy soil puts me back on top of that crumbly, mahogany-colored mountain. Breathing in earth scent while I'm weeding lets me become that little girl again, the one most in her element when mucking about in the dirt. The smell of the earth is perfume to me.

I also think my need to construct things, to work with my hands, to fix things, is a legacy from my Grandpa Hill. My grandfather grew up on a farm in Illinois and later became an automobile mechanic. His understanding of how things worked and how to fix them when they didn't got his family through the Great Depression. Weeding is a way of fixing things; you take what's gumming up the garden and yank it out, allowing the garden to function smoothly once again. First you construct a garden, and then you must maintain it.

Weeding teaches patience. I still have to stop myself, when walking tool-less through the garden, from trying to pull weeds by hand without a trowel or weeding knife to loosen the soil around the roots first. Weeds that break away at the soil level will come back stronger as the roots get the message they need to try again, even harder this time, to produce a plant that will survive. (This is why grass that's mowed comes back denser and plants that are pruned fill out more thickly.) Take time to get the right tool if you're going to bother at all.

So what happens to the weeds once they're pulled? Those that might take root and multiply in my compost go into a trash container for yard-waste pickup, but the less invasive ones go into the compost pile, where they can begin their transformation from bedeviler to benefactor. Emerson's observation that a weed is "a plant whose virtues have not been discovered"[1] seems particularly apt as I consider how many weeds have brought new life to my garden in the form of compost. Their virtue will be to act as fertilizer and soil conditioner for future gardens. Even the weeds that go into the county dump's compost hills, weeds so aggressive that I want them completely out of my life, will return in the form of mulch in a public park somewhere in my town. Nothing is wasted in a garden.

I use mulch to keep weeding down and make it easier when it's still necessary—and it always is. A layer of mulch helps prevent weeds from taking over the garden, and when a weed does manage to push through the mulch, it puts down its roots in loose, friable soil rather than the sun-baked "pottery" that soil often becomes when left exposed to the elements. Even here in my sandy Florida gardens, roots hang on more obstinately in unprotected soil. The tougher the weather and soil conditions, the more the weeds seem programmed to develop tough, tenacious root systems. Mulch keeps the soil beneath it loamy and makes weeding a more pleasurable task.

As I work my way through the garden, extracting what doesn't contribute to its health and welfare, carefully avoiding what I want to preserve, I move in the rhythm of confessional prayer. Out goes the undesirable vegetation that might take over the whole garden, and in comes the cleansing breath of fresh air and the nurturing rays of sunshine, no longer obstructed by plants that hog more than their share. Out go my own sins and shortcomings, rising on the wind of confession, and in comes amazing grace, how sweet the sound. Both garden and gardener are sanctified. As I weed my garden, I pray that the invasive plants within my own life will be uprooted, cast away, transformed into something good and wholesome. Through this weeding work, my sense of harmony is restored; I sense the balance in my life reasserting itself as order returns to the garden.

Staying Grounded

If gardening is therapy, weeding is catharsis, especially when you're upset or angry. I've often spent an hour in my garden, "worrying the bone" about some source of vexation, going through all the I-should-have-saids and the I-wish-I-hadn't-saids, while digging away at the things I can control. Weeding offers immediate gratification, especially when you unzip a long piece of Johnson grass or Virginia creeper and end up with a bushel of green from one or two operations. When I finish—exhausted in that most satisfying way, gratified by the tidy look of the beds and borders—I'm usually over my negative emotions. I'm emotionally spent but cleansed, purged of those weeds in my own spirit—the insidious, invasive, energy-sapping emotions that have no place in the garden of my soul.

As I weed, down on my knees, breathing in the sweet smell of earth, performing the work of the good gardener, and watching the lines between structure and out-of-control grow clearer, I work on weeding my own heart. I name each weakness that chokes the vitality of my spiritual life, and I assign that name to the weeds I'm pulling from my garden. Here is anger at my friend—chickweed. Here is envy—crab grass. There is laziness—dandelion. And these oxalis plants? Pride.

I stand up and look with pleasure over the newly cleaned-up garden as I enjoy the feeling of my newly shriven spirit. I look out for the volunteers—those cleome or salvia or bell pepper seedlings hiding among the unwanted plants, seedlings I would never have noticed had I not been weeding my garden. I accept these gifts from the garden as a kind of absolution, a reminder that if I name my faults and failings, root them out, and ask forgiveness, I'll receive God's cleansing grace. Grace: that gift freely given again and again, unearned and unmerited, God-offered for our spiritual pleasure, the nourishment of our souls, and a pathway back to Him. Like the freshening morning breeze, the grace of forgiveness moves over me and refreshes me. I have given something to the garden and come away the receiver of the gift.

Soul Gardening

Learn the names of the weeds in your garden, and assign each of them a name of something unproductive you're struggling with. As you root them out, visualize yourself as gaining control over each sin or shortcoming. Start thinking of weeding not as drudgery but as a way to get down and close to your garden and your plants. Use weeding as an excuse to be alone. And you'll likely be alone; rare is the friend or family member who will offer to help you weed the garden! Stand up after you've weeded a section, and admire your handiwork. Look at the cleared-out spaces around your plants, and visualize your soul being cleansed and purged of the things that keep you from being balanced and whole in your life.

25

Moonflower
Ipomoea alba

*There is something haunting in the light of the moon;
it has all the dispassionateness of a disembodied soul
and something of its inconceivable mystery.*
—Joseph Conrad, *Lord Jim*

If you've ever come upon a trellis covered with fully opened, seven-inch blooms of moonflowers "by the light of the silvery moon," you know there's magic in the night. As soon as it's dark outside, moonflowers unfurl their blossoms and remain open until touched by the morning sun. It literally takes your breath away to encounter the moonflower's glowing white face and enchantingly sweet scent on any night, but especially a moonlit one.

Moonflower vines can get as tall as twenty feet as they twine themselves around trellises, trees, or arbors. *Ipomoea alba*, as its Latin name indicates, is related to the morning glory *(Ipomoea purpurea)* and looks quite a bit like it—only it has larger leaves and blossoms. Like morning glory seeds, moonflower seeds should be soaked or nicked with a file before planting. Garden lore holds that moonflowers should be planted during the new moon, although I've had good success planting them at all times of the month.

Moonflower is native to tropical states in North America, particularly Florida, but it's now naturalized in many other tropical areas of the world. It can be grown as a perennial vine in zone nine in the south or as an annual farther north. It re-seeds freely, so even if it dies back or freezes, new volunteer seedlings are always at some stage of development around the feet of the mature vines.

Moonflower is a fast grower, able to go from a seedling to a blanket of green covering a fence or trellis in just a few months. "From curious star-shaped black calyces, which are actually used as a curry flavoring in Sri Lanka, greenish buds emerge, growing within a day or two into long green tubes ready to un-furl. And this they do with a flourish in the late afternoon or early evening, becoming giant seven-inch round flowers of the most beautiful pearly white that literally glow in the dark."[1] That description alone is enough to make even the most conventional gardener try growing moonflowers.

Another almost magical thing about moonflowers is the ra-pidity with which the flowers open. The whole blooming pro-cess, from bud to wide-open flower, often takes less than twenty minutes. If you're patient, you can see the blooms move. Bota-nists have recorded individual blooms taking less than a min-ute to fully open! And almost immediately, nocturnal insects and moths come calling, pollinating as they move from flower to flower, attracted by the moonflowers' nearly phosphorescent white color and provocative smell.

Just as the moonflower is one of my favorite night-blooming plants, my favorite insect of the night is the lime green luna moth, also named for the moon ("luna" means "moon" in Lat-in). An inhabitant of eastern North America, the luna moth *(Ac-*

tias luna) is in the family Saturniidae, which also includes giant silkworm moths. All these moths can have wingspans of almost six inches. The luna moth appears even larger, however, because of the long tails on its hind wings.

Most of the Saturnids have wings marked by "eyespots," a feature that's thought to scare off potential predators. The eyespots on the luna moth are especially noticeable because of the color of the luna's wings: a pale chartreuse that's astounding to behold. The first time I saw a luna moth was when Kurt, a biologist and partner in our back-to-the-land adventure in 1974, pointed one out to me. This miracle of winged artistry had landed on the screen door of the cabin where we lived in Schaberg Valley the first year we were in Arkansas. I guess the glow of our kerosene lanterns had attracted him. Kurt knew it was a male because of its pronounced plumose—or feathery—antennae, which, he explained, are especially large in the males of the species and are adept at picking up minute traces of pheromones—chemicals released by the female that allow males to track her down even in complete darkness.

I became so fascinated by luna moths that I researched them on my own after that. I learned that after the male and female mate, the female lays clusters of tiny black eggs that grow into caterpillars. When the eggs hatch, the caterpillars go through a series of growth stages and eventually form a papery, thin-walled cocoon on the ground.

Luna moth caterpillars reach lengths of slightly more than three inches and dine on leaves of hickories, walnuts, birches, common persimmon, and sweet gum. In the hardwood forests of the Ozark Mountains, it's not unusual to spot a luna moth, but closer into civilization they have been hurt by habitat loss. "As hardwood forests have been sacrificed to development and lost to disease, food sources for their larvae have been eliminated, and some populations have been decimated by indiscriminate spraying of pesticides."[2] Gardeners should avoid the latter and, if they wish to encourage luna moths to dwell near their gardens, should resist cutting down hickory, walnut, or persimmon trees.

For me, both the moonflower and the luna moth symbolize hope. The moonflower is a nightlight that stays on until the sun rises and may stay open even longer on a cloudy day. Even after a blossom is spent and closes up, fresh new flowers open each evening to replace the ones from the night before. The luna moth, like the moonflower, was here before the Europeans came to this country, and despite our shortsighted stewardship of the fragile things of this world, these two wonders of God's creation survive. To walk out among the moonflowers, to spot a luna moth on the window—these simple encounters with the natural world give me hope.

Maybe the moonflower and the luna moth are important to me because the wonder of the moon itself also offers hope. One summer night in 2003 the heavens featured a total lunar eclipse. Several planets were also in alignment, an anomaly that astrology aficionados called a "harmonic concordance." I went with friends to watch this special eclipse at a place where folks who would be praying for world peace were to gather. I decided to make the trip, because I thought it would be a chance to see a lunar eclipse away from the light pollution of the city as well as to see what this peace gathering was all about.

The hilltop was covered with people of all ages sitting or lying on blankets spread out on the grass. There were music, incense, and people of many faiths offering prayers for peace. But when the shadow of the earth finally began to darken the surface of the full moon, the light from so many torches, campfires, and candles obscured the clear view of the sky. I moved away from the crowd and lay alone on my blanket, looking up, wishing I were even farther from their lights so I could better experience the celestial lights on this singular night.

There is something powerful about people praying together, in whatever form and from whatever culture. I went to the gathering because I wanted to be part of a group that was outdoors looking at the moon together, thinking about God, and praying for peace in a world that knows no peace.

Our world has much need for prayers of peace. In the late 1960s I came together with others to pray for an end to the war in Vietnam. This time it was for an end to the war in the Middle East. And I'm sure that thirty years from now there will be other conflicts and other groups of people who will be praying that we might learn to "study war no more."

The Bible tells us that there will always be "wars and rumors of wars" (Matthew 24:6), because people are quick to anger and slow to forgive, greedy and self-centered. But war is a choice, not an inevitability, and as long as the world is fractured by war, all we can do is go outside at night, look at the heavens, pray for peace, and help heal this war-torn world by planting our gardens.

The first time I included bunches of white-flowering plants in my garden, I was delighted and amazed to discover that after the sun set these ethereal-looking plants continued to emanate light. It was as if sunshine had been stored in their blossoms, the way solar energy is stored in photovoltaic cells, just so they could come on after dark like solar-powered night-lights. In the moonlight the effect is particularly pronounced and startling, but even on a pitch-black night, the subtle glow of white flowers in bloom eerily lights up the garden. The night-blooming garden, especially with its moonflowers and dancing nocturnal insects like the luna moth, is a symbol of persistent hope in what seems at times to be a dark and daunting world.

26

Sharing the Bounty

Of all hobbies, gardening . . . seems to make for
generosity and good fellowship the world over;
and it is surprising how a total stranger will
share his treasures with a kindred spirit, and to what
trouble he will go to assist a fellow-gardener.
—Alice Martineau, *The Herbaceous Garden*

As a writer who spends hours alone nearly every day, I view my gardening as a conduit to the outside world. The garden is my parlor where I receive my callers, and folks who pause on their walk past the corner where my house and garden are situated will likely go away with an armful of fresh-cut flowers, a couple of ripe tomatoes, a silky purple eggplant, or a bunch of parsley, rosemary, or oregano. All a person has to do is express an interest in a particular plant to receive a cutting or be offered a seedling that has sprung up on its own and needs a home.

When I used to put in a big vegetable garden, I would give away big bags of vegetables—cucumbers, squash, tomatoes, okra—whatever I had in abundance. However, since I live in Florida, which supplies fresh vegetables to much of the country year-round, I no longer cultivate the huge vegetable gardens I once did. What I love to do is startle passersby with a Roma tomato plant right in the middle of a bunch of white dianthus and blue salvia or with a mass of scarlet runner beans growing up a trellis right alongside a honeysuckle vine. My herbs are scattered throughout all my beds and borders, both for beauty's sake and as companion plants to keep insects that don't like their smell away from the neighbor plants I want to protect. Once I even removed a border of dwarf liriope so I could plant an edging of bush beans instead—always a crowd-pleaser as well as another source of garden giving.

I used to put up a winter's worth of fruits and vegetables each summer and fall. Quart jars of scarlet spaghetti sauce, rosy gold pie apples, and amber peach halves stacked in spirals in pale pink syrup once lined my pantry shelves. Green beans, wax beans, and pinto beans stood shoulder to shoulder in their Ball Dome canning jars waiting to be used in thick soups and stews on the cold days ahead. Whenever a crop came in, whether it was from my own garden, a friend's, or a local farm, I would put up bushels of the fresh produce immediately. Canning season was ongoing and labor-intensive work. When you had a bunch of food to put up, you had to do it that day. Even twenty-four hours could affect its quality. I remember waking up in the middle of the night one year feeling waves of anxiety over some English peas I should have put up the day before but couldn't get around to. Now they were turning from their absolute prime to the beginning stages of decline, and I couldn't sleep for the knowledge.

Take corn, for example. The sugar in those crisp, sweet kernels starts turning to starch as soon the ears leave the field. Getting the corn off the cob and onto the pantry shelf or into the freezer is a huge undertaking but well worth the effort. Nothing you buy in a grocery store can compare to sweet corn that was put up just hours after being pulled from the stalk. Gardeners who understand the way food reaches its peak and then starts to lose quality put up their fruits and vegetables as soon as possible after harvest.

When I lived in Mountainburg, Arkansas, in the mid-1970s, public canneries were a big part of the economic and social life of the people. For five cents a pint and fifteen cents a quart, you could bring your own produce, jars, salt, sugar, herbs, and spices and put up your fruits and vegetables using the cannery's professional canning equipment. A bushel of apples—pared, cored, sliced, and cooked in a light sugar syrup, then poured into sterilized jars and processed in a boiling water bath for thirty minutes to kill all the bacteria—might take days to can if you did it by yourself at home. Using the cannery's huge steamers, sterilizers, water-bath processors, and pressure cookers, though, you could do the same job in an afternoon. A home canner available at a hardware store holds only seven quart jars at a time; the canners at the cannery held eighteen. And just showing up there guaranteed you would have extra hands to help with the work. Most of us couldn't afford the expensive equipment or the time needed to can at home. Few houses were air-conditioned in those days, and canning assured a rise in temperature of at least ten degrees when you did it in your own kitchen. Everything about the open-air cannery made good sense.

I remember the canneries in Mountainburg and Winslow as places to visit with neighbors and make new friends. Everyone was there for the same reason, and while your batch of applesauce was in the processor, you had nothing on your hands but time to help someone else shell field peas. If you were canning tomatoes, other folks would pitch in with blanching your tomatoes to slip off the skins and packing them into hot, sterilized jars while their own cans of collard greens were being processed in the pressure canner. While your tomatoes boiled away in sealed jars in the water bath, you would help someone else ladle blackberry preserves into pint jars. Friends and strangers traded their excess produce with each other, and often by the end of the day each person went home with a variety of jams, sauces, condiments, pie fillings, and vegetables. Sharing the newly preserved wealth of the garden and field was as much a part of gardening as helping one another with the process of what was then called "putting food by." It was all about saving, conserving, preserving, and sharing the bounty.

It was only after the huge warehouse stores and supermarkets came into the back country that people started buying more factory-processed canned goods and canning less of their own produce. As use of the canneries declined, so did politicians' interest in funding them at the state and county levels. Today canneries are a thing of the past, not even worthy of an entry in the historical records of the counties where they were once such an important part of community life.

Part of living in community is doing one's part to make the world more beautiful. Besides turning me into a gardener, my years in Arkansas have blessed—or cursed—me with an incurable compulsion to reduce, reuse, recycle. I still rinse out and reuse those inexpensive plastic resealable storage bags until they sport holes. Most folks I know toss them away after only one use, although those with a more highly developed ecological consciousness recycle them at the grocery. Like the public canneries I remember so fondly, the idea of washing and reusing plastic bags and containers has become passé, almost quaint, no longer a part of most people's lifestyle.

Gardening makes you aware of the effort and energy that go into producing and preserving even the most humble food. I still use whatever food I have until it's practically unrecognizable, and then what's left gets recycled into the compost pile. The other day I got a call from my neighbor John asking if he could put into my compost pile some potatoes that were going bad. He said he would leave the whole bag of them in the wheelbarrow in my backyard, and I could decide whether to compost or throw them into the trash. Instead of either, I picked through the potatoes, finding only about five small rotten ones that were spoiling the whole bunch, and used the nearly three pounds of Yukon golds that were left to make a garlic potato–cheese casserole. The five bad ones *did* go into the compost pile, but the good ones made a delicious side dish that I shared with John. Sharing the bounty goes on in many different guises.

Staying Grounded

Gardeners are productive and conservative at the same time. The work that goes into production makes us appreciate what we grow and want to preserve and share it. We experience a great deal of satisfaction from being creative, and we enjoy sharing the results of that creativity. Non-gardeners don't always understand that, for us, gardening is not only work but an art form: it's something we want to do with our time and energy. We reduce consumption, reuse whatever still has use in it, and recycle by composting wastes and sharing what we grow.

This need to create, to feel satisfaction in what's created, and to share that creation with others—isn't this also what spiritual growth is about? We have a need to grow closer to God. When we mature spiritually, we change. And as we change, we have a desire to share our new awareness with others. We can't help ourselves. That's what artists do, that's what gardeners do, and that's what people who are seeking spiritual growth do.

Soul Gardening

If you're a gardener, you already share the beauty of your garden with everyone who sees what you do. In the morning, when you lay your requests before God and wait in expectation, think about practical ways you can give to others from the bounty of your life. In what ways has the generosity of others influenced you?

27

Letting It Rest

Six days you shall labor, but on the seventh day you shall rest; even during the plowing season and harvest you must rest.
—Exodus 34:21

My husband laughed when I told him that the title of the final task chapter in this book was "Letting It Rest." I confess up front that of all the things I preach about gardening, this is the most difficult one for me to practice. I started out writing about how I go outside every morning with my coffee and stroll through the garden looking at all that my labors the previous day wrought, enjoying the beauty I help create.

But even as I was writing those words, I knew I was kidding myself. I am not *resting* when I walk through my garden: I'm taking note of what needs to be pruned, of how a certain plant would look so much better over there, of where I need to concentrate my weeding energy next time I have an hour to spend maintaining the garden.

We all know that whenever our minds are racing around with concerns about what we have to do in the next hour or the next day, it's almost impossible to get a good night's sleep, let alone feel peaceful when we wake up. Rest isn't just sitting there doing nothing; true rest is allowing the cares and concerns of life to blow over and away from us. True rest means not processing the next job or the next chore or the next responsibility. Resting is much more about trust than control, and that's where the gardener often has the most trouble.

Here also, we can learn a lot from our gardens. The land, like all living things, needs time to rest. Nature provides ways for the land to recover its energy while lying fallow, and one of the miracles of nature is nitrogen-fixing bacteria. I remember when I first learned about nitrogen-fixing bacteria in my tenth-grade biology class. The idea that certain nodes on certain legumes or grasses have the ability to pull nitrogen out of the air and "fix" it into the soil as fertilizer seemed miraculous to me. It's like the way the heart and lungs work in the human body, taking in oxygen and releasing carbon dioxide back into the atmosphere. Then green plants take that CO_2 and transform it back into oxygen. Can anyone truly study the laws of nature and not believe in a divine hand behind the design and engineering of this remarkable planet?

So we get to the point where adding fertilizers and compost and mulch is just not enough. It's time to take a part of the garden and plant it in alfalfa or soybeans for a season. Then after a year of rest, we can dig that green manure back into the soil in order to replenish and restore it to health. It's good for the garden, and it's good for the gardener. What a relief to put, say, a third of the garden to bed for a season! It's that much less work for us, and watching that patch of brown green over with a life-giving cover crop connects us both to the earth and to the people who have been practicing this technique for as far back as we have agricultural records. Communities that did not understand the need for letting the land rest paid the price. They themselves could never rest, because, moving from one fertile place they had literally depleted to death to a new, fertile place, they were forever starting over. These were nomadic people.

Those who stayed put had to learn to let the land take a break and recover its energy every few years. And those of us who choose to stay put and work our own little corner of the earth have to learn to do this too.

"Staying put" is hard for me—I love a new project. It drives my husband crazy, because we can be talking about replacing a leaky faucet, and within five minutes I'm drawing up plans for remodeling the bathroom. The happiest years of my younger days were when I worked the hardest at building, landscaping, gardening, cooking, canning, sewing, doing needlework, raising chickens. It makes me tired just to think about it! But that's who I am: someone who gets energy from putting out energy, and I fulfill my need to be creative by creating.

Gardeners, like all people who love what they do, can become workaholics. Much has been written about gardening as therapy, but therapy can become an addiction too. I feel healthiest in my garden, most productive, more creative than just about anywhere else in my world. I feel closer to God there, too, and that's where the resting part comes in. I—and perhaps you, too—need to learn to be in the garden without always *working* in the garden, no matter how satisfying the work.

In the Book of Deuteronomy, written about thirty-four hundred years ago, the author tells how the Israelites were commanded by God to rest from all their labors every seventh day. Most of us are familiar with the commandment to "observe the Sabbath day by keeping it holy. . . . Six days you shall labor and do all your work, but the seventh day is a Sabbath to the LORD your God. On it you shall not do any work" (Deuteronomy 5:12-14). But few people realize that in ancient times every seventh year was to be a sabbatical as well. The Israelites were instructed not to plant their fields but to live off whatever the land provided for them on its own. "For six years sow your fields, and for six years prune your vineyards and gather their crops. But in the seventh year . . . the land is to have a year of rest. Whatever the land yields during the Sabbath year will be food for you" (Leviticus 25:3-6).

In other words, the people were to become hunters and gatherers for a year and give the land a rest. God promised to provide enough food in this Sabbath year by sending them an overabundance in the sixth year:

> You may ask, "What will we eat in the seventh year if we do not plant or harvest our crops?" I will send you such a blessing in the sixth year that the land will yield enough for three years. While you plant during the eighth year, you will eat from the old crop and will continue to eat from it until the harvest of the ninth year comes in" *(Leviticus 25:20-22).*

These people were asked to trust God to meet their needs, even while they let the land have a rest.

I wonder if it was as hard for the Israelites to stay out of their gardens as it is for me. And why, I wonder, is it so hard to trust God to run the universe and not feel personally responsible for making things happen? Resting is about trusting that the world will go on without our having a hand in making it happen.

Staying Grounded

Take a look at any self-help section in a bookstore, and note how many books are on learning to relax and to "be in the moment." Why do you think this is such a hot topic? Maybe because the world is "too much with us," and we've become convinced that work is good and that relaxing is goofing off. So we need books that tell us otherwise. A strong work ethic—the idea that anyone who works hard enough can achieve almost anything in life—is the foundation and backbone of our society.

But it takes only an objective look at reality to see that this theory is full of holes, because people born into lower socio-economic groups are at a disadvantage in achieving what the United States calls the American dream. Still, the illusion persists that anyone who's not successful in our culture must not be working hard enough.

People who spend even a small amount of time in front of a television set are bombarded by "gotta have it" advertisements that feed our greed and "need" to acquire possessions. Even though spending money to keep up with whatever is in style this year is counterintuitive to the notion of accumulating wealth, both result in the same dilemma: people spend most of their waking hours working to earn money to buy things that take *more* money to store and to maintain, so they have to work harder to take care of all the things they own. The further irony is that these expensive toys are supposed to be for our leisure time, the time we rest and relax, but that resting time shrinks in proportion to the debt we accumulate as we purchase our stuff. We're programmed by both our families and the popular culture to make money, and that means working.

One of the few ways to get off this treadmill is to practice the art of resting. If that means scheduling a nap at noon, then we need to do it if possible. If it means taking seriously the admonition to, like the lilies of the field, "neither spin nor toil" (and that includes working in the garden) one day a week, then so be it. I wonder if in the days when people didn't do anything but read the Bible on Sundays, there wasn't a deep-seated realization that we have to force ourselves to stop, to read words of wisdom, to nap, to unwind, to relax. We have to schedule time to rest just as we have to schedule time to work.

Like the field left fallow for a season so that it will be more productive when it's put back to work again, we must not only *allow* but *schedule* fallow time for ourselves. We must learn to trust that when we rest, we're restocking our creative ponds, fertilizing our productive fields. We're practicing the art of being still, and in that stillness the words, the energy, and the power to do what needs doing are rekindled and renewed.

Soul Gardening

Give yourself—and your garden—a break. Decide to take one small section of your garden and let it lie fallow for a year. Then plan how you will give yourself some fallow time every week. Mark this time in your day planner or calendar, and treat it as you would any other appointment. Relearn the leisurely art of napping. Then pay attention to how you feel during and after your resting time. See if by giving yourself permission to be still you don't have more energy and a better attitude during the times you're busy and productive.

28

Yesterday-Today-and-Tomorrow
Brunfelsia pauciflora *"Floribunda"*

To have been placed on this earth "to dress and keep it"
was the divine intention; to make it a garden of
delights for ourselves and our children where the
healthy prodding and stirring of the soil should
produce, not only nourishing fruit for the body,
but also most nourishable food for the mind.
—Augustine, *City of God*

You are a gardener, or you want to be one, or you know someone who is a gardener—otherwise you would not have picked up this book. Even if you have yet to turn over your first shovelful of sod, even if you've planted gardens only in your mind so far, even if you're just beginning to do something about this need you have to play in the dirt and make things grow, there lurks within you a gardener waiting to be born.

If you're already a gardener, you know certain things.

You know there's a profound connection between being human and tending a garden. You believe God is both Creator and Artist; the longer you've been a gardener, the surer you've become of this. By virtue of your witnessing the process of life, death, and rebirth on a daily basis, you share with other gardeners this conviction: the natural world with all its complexity, beauty, and wonder is no accident. You know a guiding hand set it all in motion and invites you to participate in its continuation. That's being a person of *faith*.

You also know that there are those who feel a calling that's almost a compulsion to work the earth and to create beauty where, left to its own devices, there would be only barrenness and desolation or, at best, sameness and uniformity. You're by nature a producer and a designer, and this shows up in other aspects of your life besides gardening. You know that gardening is in your soul, that it's a need and a calling. That's called having a *passion*.

You know, too, that you're drawn to being outdoors rather than inside, that you need to stand and look at what you've accomplished, admire it and feel the satisfaction that comes from having something lovely to show for your time and talents. You also know that you can't look for long without getting a new idea for yet another garden project and that you look at every yard and garden you pass and think, *I should plant some of those in front of my hydrangeas.* That's called being a *visionary*.

Gardening answers that need to express our artistic ability, to feel close to the earth, to connect with the dust from which we came and to which we'll return, and to be "closer to God in the garden than anyplace else on earth," as Dorothy Frances Gurney said. That's called having *hope*.

You know these things, and you are these things, because you're a gardener. Or perhaps you're a gardener because you have faith, passion, vision, and hope, and these aspects need an outlet. Being a gardener assigns you to a way of life that centers on the cycles of nature. Gardening has no real beginning and no end. Passersby will comment on how great your gardens look. Then they'll ask, "How do you keep at it? You never really get to *finish*, do you?" The answers are "Because I love it" and "No." And that's okay with you.

As we work outside doing the many things gardeners do, it can appear to non-gardeners that we're slaves to a series of endless chores. What they don't understand is that we like it that way. Some people become energized from rearranging their furniture, remodeling their homes, or buying new clothes, cars, and other toys. We who are called to the garden are enlivened by change, growth, and surprise. Like God's great compassion, our gardens are "new every morning" (Lamentations 3:23).

But you understand all this. You're one of the fortunate ones whose calling is to garden. Most gardeners confess to having wanted to garden for as long as they can remember. Once they finally find a way to make gardening part of their lives, they do it almost daily, and they'll be doing it in some capacity for as long as they can lift a trowel. To garden is to be a part of the past, the present, and the future.

Yesterday-Today-and-Tomorrow

In the shady courtyard gardens of old Savannah, Georgia, pots and urns overflow with the luxuriant plant called yesterday-today-and-tomorrow. Its flowers appear to come in three colors—deep purple, lavender, and white—but actually each blossom starts out purple and changes colors daily for the three days it blooms. Thus its name. What's lavender today was purple yesterday and will be white tomorrow.

Yesterday-today-and-tomorrow thrives in warm climates, but it will grow anywhere as a potted plant, which can be taken indoors in the winter. For that matter, if I lived north of zone eight, I would grow it as an annual each year. The price of replacement every spring would be well worth the expense, and as it seeds freely, you can even start your own plants from last year's parent plant. Yesterday-today-and-tomorrow is covered with flowers throughout the growing season, and it can grow as large as five feet tall. It is usually pruned back into a more compact habit that encourages leafing and blooming. This treatment makes it an excellent plant for outdoor pots and window boxes.

The name of this plant and its parti-colored flowers remind me to be aware of time and its passage. This year in particular, the meaning of time has altered for me as dramatically as a blossom turning from purple to lavender to white.

As I mentioned earlier, my father—absent by his choice for the past two decades—came back into my life, old and needy and in the beginning stages of Alzheimer's disease. My mother, who was my best friend, died suddenly of lung cancer a few months later. During this time several people close to me have been undergoing treatments for life-threatening illnesses, and the treatments are almost as scary as what they're attempting to cure. Mortality is sighting me down its barrel.

I know that physical decline and death are inevitable. What strikes me as significant right now, however, is the way my yesterdays, todays, and tomorrows all seem to be merging at the most unexpected times.

In the middle of sorting piles of papers one afternoon, I uncovered at the bottom of a box of odds and ends a letter I had written to my mother when I lived in Arkansas. Suddenly I was taken out of the present and into the past.

Then I got a call from the assisted-living facility where my father is a resident, and I stopped everything to attend to his present needs.

Later I wrote in my journal about whether the treatment is killing the virus in my friend's bloodstream—and if not, what then? Before I know it, I'm worrying about the future.

But in the garden I find a timelessness that isn't confusing or sad or frightening. Gardening keeps me centered and grounded in the present; it's the best way I know to stay in the *now.* If the new transplants are wilting from lack of water, they need me right now, this minute. If weeds are choking out tiny seedlings that have been struggling to assert themselves, I can't wait around to see which one wins. It's my job and my joy to get outside and make things right in the garden *today.*

The garden also ties me to my past and to my mother, who kept a garden everywhere she lived and who modeled what it meant to love gardening. I brush past the rosemary bush, and the piney-sweet fragrance rises to meet me. Rosemary *(Rosmarinus officinalis)* is an ancient symbol of remembrance. The ancients believed it strengthened the memory, and it became an emblem of commemorating those who have died. *Rosemary for remembrance,* I think, feeling the sadness of knowing my mother will never again walk through my gardens with me, enjoying all the sights, sounds, and smells or praising the results of my labor. Yet with that remembrance comes not only sorrow but joy. The act of gardening ties me to my mother and to all the generations of gardeners who came before her, whose blood flows in my veins, whose love of the earth lives on in me. It binds me to my *yesterdays.*

And *tomorrow?* Every morning is a new beginning, a chance to see what happened in the garden overnight. I awake in anticipation of checking to see if the new transplants, after ten hours of darkness and dew, are a little stronger and stouter than the day before. I wake before the sunrise, impatient for the sky to lighten enough for me to step out onto my lawn and see how the weeding and deadheading and mulching I did yesterday look today. As my eyes scan the landscape through the steam from my coffee, I'm already planning what I can do to make my garden even better tomorrow.

Gardeners have a ministry of flowers, fruit, vegetables, and herbs. Our work reminds others that we're a part of this earth on which we spend our todays and our yesterdays and to which, some bright tomorrow, our bodies will return. In the meantime, if God and nature bless our efforts, our gardens will give hope and beauty to this sometimes sad and wicked world. As a gardener, you're part of that hope, a keeper of the wisdom in growing things.

Notes

Preface

1. Margaret Silf, foreword to Vigen Guroian, *Inheriting Paradise: Meditations of Gardening* (Grand Rapids: William B. Eerdmans, 1999), vii.

Chapter 1

1. Franky Schaeffer, *Addicted to Mediocrity: 20th Century Christians and the Arts* (Westchester, Ill.: Cornerstone Books, 1981), 57.

Chapter 3

1. Stuart Maddox Masters, *The Seasons Through* (London: H. Jenkins, 1948), 23.

2. Ibid., 25.

Chapter 5

1. Smith & Hawken, *The Book of Outdoor Gardening* (New York: Workman Publishing, 1996), 217.

Chapter 6

1. William Wordsworth, "The World Is Too Much with Us," line 1.

2. Robert Herrick, "To the Virgins to Make Much of Time," lines 1–4.

Chapter 7

1. Laura C. Martin, *Garden Flower Folklore* (Chester, Conn.: Globe Pequot Press, 1987), 133.

Chapter 12

1. James Underwood Crockett, *Crockett's Victory Garden* (Boston: Little, Brown, 1977), 66.

Chapter 13

1. Thomas Moore, "Believe Me, If All Those Endearing Young Charms," in *The Golden Book of Favorite Songs,* comp. John W. Beattie et al. (Chicago: Hall & McCreary, 1923), 46.

Chapter 14

1. "Manure tea" is a solution of water and composted animal manure that can be poured directly onto plants as fertilizer.

Chapter 19

1. Gregg Pasterick, "Wildflowers of North America: Fits of Poetry and Evening-primrose," Suite101.com, <www.suite101.com/article.cfm/13513/101351>.

Chapter 20

1. Mark Nelson with Hank Bruce, *Nelson's Guide to Florida Roses* (Orlando, Fla.: Waterview Press, 2003).

Chapter 21

1. Smith and Hawken, *The Book of Outdoor Gardening,* 239.

2. Albert Einstein, Thinkexist.com, <http://en.thinkexist.com/search/searchquotation.asp?search=einstein>.

Chapter 23

1. Catriona Tudor Erler, *The Frugal Gardener: How to Have More Garden for Less Money* (Emmaus, Pa.: Rodale Press, 1999), 164.

Chapter 24

1. Ralph Waldo Emerson, *The Fortune of the Republic and Other American Addresses,* Riverside Literature Series (Boston: Houghton Mifflin, 1889).

Chapter 25

1. "Moonflower," Buena Creek Gardens, <http://www.buenacreek gardens.com/moonflower.htm>.

2. "Big Green Monster?" Hilton Pond Center for Piedmont Natural History, http://www.hiltonpond.org/ThisWeek020801.html>.

Bibliography

Chaplin, Lois Frigg. *Annuals*. Birmingham, Ala.: Oxmore House, 1996.

Crockett, James Underwood. *Crockett's Victory Garden*. Boston: Little, Brown, 1977.

Gail, Peter. *The Delightfully Delicious Daylily: Recipes and More*. Cleveland: Goosefoot Acres Press, 1989.

Martin, Laura C. *Garden Flower Folklore*. Chester, Conn.: Globe Pequot Press, 1987.

Masters, Maddox. *The Seasons Through*. London: H. Jenkins, 1948.

Nelson, Mark, with Hank Bruce. *Nelson's Guide to Florida Roses*. Orlando, Fla.: Waterview Press, 2003.

Overbeck, Cynthia. *Sunflowers*. Minneapolis: Learner Publications, 1981.

Perényi, Eleanor. *Green Thoughts: A Writer in the Garden*. 2002 Modern Library Edition. New York: Modern Library Garden, 2002.

Philip Lief Group, Inc. *The National Gardening Association Dictionary of Horticulture*. New York: Penguin Books, 1996.

Schaeffer, Franky. *Addicted to Mediocrity: 20th Century Christians and the Arts* Westchester, Ill.: Cornerstone Books, 1981.

Smith & Hawkins. *The Book of Outdoor Gardening*. New York: Workman Publishing, 1996.

About the Author

Janice Elsheimer is a writer and speaker who teaches gifted children part-time in order to support her gardening habit. Her award-winning first book, *The Creative Call,* invites adults to see the reawakening of their creative talents as an opportunity for spiritual growth. The popularity of the book has propelled her into a speaking and consulting business that keeps her away from her garden more than she would like. She enjoys tending her "bit of earth" in Winter Park, Florida, where she lives with her husband, Seth.

Find time to refresh and renew your relationship with God.

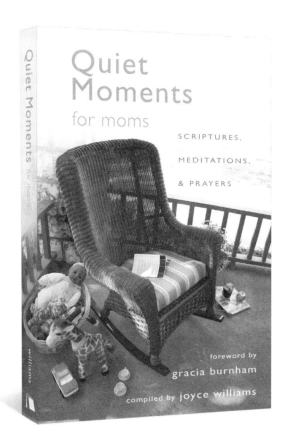

With experiences and insights from other moms, these devotionals will help you focus on the strength and power of God as you find rest and comfort in the midst of motherhood's many challenges.

Quiet Moments for Moms
Scriptures, Meditations, and Prayers
Compiled by Joyce Williams
ISBN: 978-0-8341-2355-7

BEACON HILL PRESS
OF KANSAS CITY

Available online and wherever books are sold.

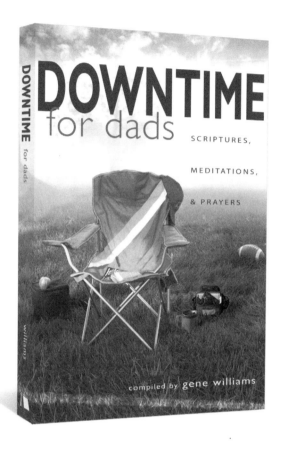